REMEMBER WHEN

IDEALS PUBLISHING CORPORATION
NASHVILLE, TENNESSEE

REMEMBER WHEN

PHOTOGRAPHS

2-3, Old Victrola, Gerald Koser; 4, God Bless Our Home, Gerald Koser; 6, Teakettle and Bread, Gerald Koser; 8-9, Winter Clothesline, H. Armstrong Roberts; 10, Mixing Bowl, Gerald Koser; 12, Ice Cream Freezer, Gerald Koser; 14, Colored Glassware, Gerald Koser; 16, Cider Press, Gerald Koser; 18, Boy at Pump, H. Armstrong Roberts; 21, Mother's Kitchen, Gerald Koser; 22, Hay Rake in Snow, Harold M. Lambert Studios; 24, Memories, J. Amos/H. Armstrong Roberts; 27, Homemade Pie, Gerald Koser; 28, Sledding Boy, H. Armstrong Roberts; 30, Harvesting Hay, H. Armstrong Roberts; 33, Old Buttons, FPG; 34, Sweet Shop, Mary Jane Hayes; 36, Braided Pillow, Gerald Koser; 38, Washboard, H. Armstrong Roberts; 41, Radio and Lamp, Ralph Luedtke; 43, Evening Games, Gerald Koser; 44-45, Family Gathering, H. Armstrong Roberts; 46, Family Album, Gerald Koser; 48, Crocheted Picture Frame, Gerald Koser; 50, Old Toys, Gerald Koser; 53, Rain Barrel, Gerald Koser; 54, Shooting Marbles, H. Armstrong Roberts; 56, Porcelain Doll, Gerald Koser; 58, School Supplies, Gerald Koser; 61, Desk and Letters, Gerald Koser; 63, Old Typewriter, Gebhardt/H. Armstrong Roberts; 64, Old-Fashioned Picnic, Gerald Koser; 66, Tiptoe over Rocks, Harold M. Lambert Studios; 68, Baseball Memorabilia, Al Riccio; 71, Front Porch, Gerald Koser; 73, Neighbor's House, Gerald Koser; 74, Haystacks, H. Armstrong Roberts; 77, Grocery Shelves, L. Fritz/H. Armstrong Roberts; 78, Neighborhood Drugstore, Gerald Koser; 80, S. S. Kresge, The Bettmann Archive; 82, The General Store, Gerald Koser; 84, Hometown Street, Gerald Koser; 86, Historic Town Clock, Dubuque, Iowa, H. Armstrong Roberts; 88, Movie House, Old Milwaukee Museum, Ralph Luedtke; 91, Movie Poster, The Bettmann Archive; 93, Town Band, Green Bay, Wisconsin, H. Armstrong Roberts; 94, Old Church, Gerald Koser; 96, Old Assembly Building, courtesy Monteagle Sunday School Assembly, Monteagle, Tennessee; 99, Circus Wagon, Ralph Luedtke; 100, Carrousel, H. Armstrong Roberts; 102, Old Highways, P. Wallick/H. Armstrong Roberts; 104, Visiting Grandma, H. Armstrong Roberts; 106, Covered Bridge, Ralph Luedtke; 108-109, Steam Locomotive, The Bettmann Archive; 111, Boarding the Train, H. Armstrong Roberts; 112-113, San Francisco Trolley, The Bettmann Archive; 115, Ferris Wheel, The Bettmann Archive; 116, Old-Fashioned Car, Fred Sieb; 119, Sawmill River Parkway, New York, The Bettmann Archive; 120, Bridal Veil and Mementoes, H. Armstrong Roberts; 123, Handiwork, Gerald Koser; 125, One-Room Schoolhouse, Ken Dequaine; 126, Square Dance, The Bettmann Archive; 129, Old Music, Gerald Koser; 130, Purse and Corsage, Gerald Koser; 133, Big Band, The Bettmann Archive; 135, Bridal Jewelry, Gerald Koser; 137, Wedding Day, Photographer Unknown; 138, Old Albums, Gerald Koser; 140, Holiday Postcards, Robert Flanagan; 143, Valentine Box, Gerald Koser; 144, Easter Postcards, Robert Flanagan; 146, May Basket, D. Petku/H. Armstrong Roberts; 149, Flowers on Chair, Jansen/H. Armstrong Roberts; 151, Kate Smith, H. Armstrong Roberts; 152, Horseshoes, Gerald Koser; 155, Harvesttime, Gerald Koser; 157, Hat, Mittens, and Scarf, Gerald Koser; 158, Sleigh Ride at Christmas, H. Armstrong Roberts.

An Old Friend, by Edgar A. Guest. Used by permission of the estate.

IDEALS PUBLISHING CORPORATION
NASHVILLE, TENNESSEE

Text set in Goudy; Display type set in Goudy Bold Italic; Chapter titles set in Benguiat Bold

Publisher, Patricia A. Pingry; Editor, Nancy J. Skarmeas; Book Designer, Patrick McRae

Color separations by Rayson Films, Waukesha, Wisconsin; Printed and bound by Ringier America, Brookfield, Wisconsin

CONTENTS

JOURNEY HOME

again to the taste of fresh-baked bread warm from the oven and the cool sweetness of homemade ice cream, to the comforting warmth of an old iron radiator and the welcoming sound of a teakettle whistling on the old cookstove.

Sentimental Journey
Bud Green, Les Brown & Ben Homer

Gon-na take a sen-ti-men-tal jour-ney

Gon-na set my heart at ease ~ Gon-na make a

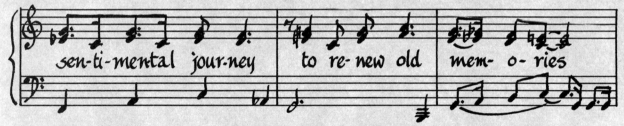

sen-ti-mental jour-ney to re-new old mem-o-ries

Nev-er thought my heart could be so "yearn-y" Why did I de-

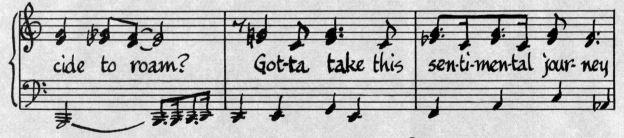

cide to roam? Got-ta take this sen-ti-men-tal jour-ney

sen-ti-men-tal jour-ney home.   FIN.

Electricity was adapted for cooking in 1914; but electric stoves did not become popular until the twenties. Even then, most families got by with a wood-burning cookstove. The teakettle, thus, was a fixture in the American kitchen, and its whistle the most reliable signal that the fire was hot enough for cooking.

The Singing Teakettle

In the old days, a singing teakettle made home more cheery and inviting.
It was there to let us know that there was a good, warm fire going,
and that a cup of hot tea was only moments away.
A singing teakettle purring happily on a stove made things merry and bright;
with every puff of steam from its spout a busy teakettle
sent out messages of good things to come. For the housewife who prepared her
dinners on a wood-burning cookstove, the teakettle signaled when the fire was
hot enough for cooking. Its magical sound soothed ill or fretting children
and convinced restless cats and dogs to snuggle down into sleep.
A singing teakettle was a friendly companion; coming home to its
humming refrain was sweetly inviting.

The homes of my yesterdays always had a teakettle
humming contentedly on the back of the stove. And today, my favorite teakettle
remains with me; for a new house is never truly a "home"
until the teakettle has begun to hum its familiar, happy tune—
I dare say, it is almost like one of the family!

Helen Colwell Oakley
New Milford, Pennsylvania

Dear Old Radiators

On the coldest days of winter, I think back to growing up in the twenties and thirties, when our rooms were warmed by big, old-fashioned iron radiators. During the summer they were barely noticed; but in the winter our iron giants came alive, keeping us warm while the wind and cold rattled the shutters and shook the house.

Radiators spread their warmth through every part of our lives. They dried our wet mittens, readying them for another round of snowman-making or another sled ride. They took the icy stiffness out of sheets and clothes dried on a winter clothesline, making them limp enough to fold. We dried diapers on top of warm radiators, and snuggled winter-born babies in pillow-filled baskets up close to their warmth. Puppies and kittens cuddled in blankets in boxes at the radiator's feet; flannel nighties warmed there while we bravely plunged into a shivery bath.

At night the big fire in the cellar was banked and the radiators cooled until they were only faintly warm by morning. While we kids were still in bed, Grandpa stirred up the coals and heaped fuel on the fire; soon the radiators were hissing and rumbling again, ready for the day. Grandma laid our long underwear and stockings on them each morning so we could jump from our cold beds into warm clothes.

In these days of automation—thermostats that control the temperature to the exact degree, twenty-four hours a day—I remember those old iron giants of my childhood with a warm and grateful heart.

Jane Baumann
Waverly, Ohio

The first automatic clothes dryer went on sale in 1946; before then, the clothesline did the job of drying laundry. Today, nostalgia for the "good old days" might inspire longing for the fresh scent of clothes dried on the line on a warm and breezy June day, but few of us would be willing to revive the clothesline in the dead of winter, when clothes went from the line directly to the radiator to relieve their icy stiffness.

Homemade bread is something of a novelty today, not yet a lost art, but certainly a disappearing one. Before the spread of chain supermarkets, however, homemade bread was not a matter of choice, but of necessity. At least one morning a week found the women of the house up with the dawn, mixing and kneading and baking breads for family meals.

Mama's Mixing Bowl

Most days the cream-colored earthenware bowl with the bold, blue stripes sits idle, a charming decoration atop my kitchen cabinet. Time was when that familiar dish served an indispensable purpose in our family's daily routine.

Every weekday morning, Mom was in the kitchen by 5:30, making biscuit dough. I can still see her now, busily sifting the flour, stirring in the milk, and kneading the sticky mixture into a smooth ball. With quick, deft movements, Mom cut the rounded biscuits and placed them carefully onto a baking pan. After drizzling them with bacon drippings or melted butter, she popped her daily handiwork into the oven. Within moments her hungry brood had devoured her labor of love. Mom kept bakery bread on hand, but only for making lunches; freshly baked biscuits always accompanied breakfast. And that wasn't all that emerged out of that old mixing bowl. Chewy oatmeal cookies, fragrant loaves of bread, batches of doughnuts, savory dumplings, and more all began in Mama's bowl with the bright blue stripes

One day not long ago, feeling a bit nostalgic, I asked my mother if she still had the old mixing bowl. She smiled and told me that, yes, she still had it, even used it on special occasions. I told her that if she ever found she didn't need it to let me know. The next week, Mama handed over the nearly fifty-year-old mixing bowl.

Although I have never matched Mama's skills in the kitchen, I do now understand the fulfillment she received providing for her family's most basic needs. And now, with family of my own, and Mama's old mixing bowl for inspiration, I realize that her secret was really no secret at all, just a dash of tender, loving care blended into each one of her recipes.

Brenda West
Roderfield, West Virginia

In the days before supermarket freezers stocked ice cream in every imaginable flavor, homemade ice cream was a cherished summertime treat. Set in motion by the arrival of the iceman with a specially ordered, giant-sized block, making ice cream required the strength and cooperation of the entire family to crush the ice and turn the crank the proper speed for the required length of time to create the sweet, creamy concoction.

Homemade Ice Cream

The new electric freezers
Are cleverly designed,
But they will never equal
The good, old-fashioned kind.

Mother had a formula
For our homemade ice cream,
Fresh eggs, sugar, cream, and things
That made it taste supreme.

Dad knew the right proportions
Of crushed ice and rock salt;
We all took turns at cranking;
At last we had to halt.

We licked the spoon and paddle,
And packed it down to set;
The memory of those good times
Still lingers with me yet.

Rachel Van Creme
Williamstown, West Virginia

The colorful, iridescent glassware mass-produced by American factories in the first part of this century is often referred to as carnival glass. Its popularity was inspired by the rise of the Tiffany lamp, which was out of the price range of the average American. Colored glassware, created by pouring molten glass into a mold, pressing it with a plunger, and treating it with a chemical mixture to create the distinctive colors, was a beautiful, affordable alternative.

Colored Glassware

I love the lovely colored glass
The old-time factories made
In pinks and greens and golds and reds
And blues of grandest shades.

The ruby red is deep, deep red,
Most splendid to behold,
For the formula for ruby glass
Used additives of gold.

There is another shade of glass
That blends both golds and greens
Into a very special tone
That's known as "vaseline."

Uranium, the additive,
That helped provide this shade
Is used no more in factories
Where modern glass is made.

The tones of pink are delicate;
I love the cobalt blue;
The purple glass reminds me of
Old friends, and old times, too.

Old colored glass speaks proudly of
The years that now have passed,
Today its called "collectible,"
Like all good things that last.

Craig E. Sathoff
Iowa Falls, Iowa

Today, a bountiful fall crop of apples rarely inspires cooks to make apple butter. But fifty years ago, the spicy-sweet spread was an autumn ritual. Homemakers even had a special tool for stirring their apple butter. Called an apple butter stick, it was made out of hickory wood and shaped much like a hoe, except with holes that made possible stirring slowly through the thick mixture for hours on end.

Old-Fashioned Apple Butter

It seems that nobody makes apple butter anymore. Perhaps we have all forgotten the wonderful, spicy taste of warm apple butter on homemade bread; more likely, too many of us are put off by the memory of the big, black kettle and the long hours of peeling and stirring. This is unfortunate. Certainly it is not convenient to peel four pounds of apples. And yes, it is time consuming to stir the mixture— sometimes for hours—until it is the right consistency. But these objections are the products of the modern mind. Think old-fashioned. Remember the pleasures of long days in the kitchen with mother or grandmother, and the shared satisfaction of a job well done. Remember that nothing tastes like good, old-fashioned home cooking, and that a day's worth of work in September can provide the unmistakable taste of apple butter through the long winter. Remember all of this, and then sit down and start peeling.

For apple butter the way it used to be, peel and core four pounds of apples. I always use Jonathan apples, but any fruit with a strong flavor will do. Cook these slowly in two cups of water in an open kettle until they are soft, and then pour the mixture through a fine strainer; you don't want to lose pulp, only water. Measure the remaining pulp and put it back into the kettle, adding a half-cup of sugar for every cup of pulp. Then add the spices—a teaspoon of cinnamon, a half-teaspoon of cloves, a quarter-teaspoon of allspice, just a touch of grated lemon rind, and a couple of squeezes of lemon juice.

Cook the mixture over low heat until the sugar is dissolved, stirring constantly. Continue cooking and stirring until the mixture thickens. You can tell it is done when no rim of liquid forms around a small amount placed on a flat dish. Serve as is on biscuits, muffins, or bread; store the rest in sterilized jars for the months ahead

And on a cold winter's day when apples and apple pies are things of the past, take down a jar of apple butter and taste the autumn, and the fruits of your old-fashioned labors.

Lucile S. MacDonald
Canterbury, New Hampshire

In the twenties and thirties many families had running water, but just as many relied on the old-fashioned pump for cooking, washing, and bathing—or simply for cool, refreshing relief from summertime heat.

A Magical Pump and an Old Crank Phone

When I was six years old, I left my home in modern Cincinnati and went to live on my aunt and uncle's family farm in Indiana. The farm was a magical place to a city girl; the horses, cows, pigs, and chickens amused me, and I marvelled at the sight of fields of wheat and corn stretching as far as the horizon. They had no electricity; only kerosene lamps in sparkling clean globes lit our rooms in the evening. Running water came from an iron pump on the back porch. When the long handle was pumped up and down it made a wonderful squeaking sound. The water that came out smelled sharp and tasted of metal, but I loved its freshness and I thrilled at the novelty of the pump.

Inside Auntie's kitchen was more magic, in the form of an old crank phone— a simple wooden box mounted on the wall with a crank on one side. Turning the crank produced a loud, jangling ring; a half turn made a short ring, a full turn one twice as long. One turned the crank a certain number of short or long turns to reach the desired party; but everyone who had a phone heard the rings, and everyone who heard the rings picked up their phone. When my father called long distance there were so many listeners on the line that the power was drained and our voices weakened. The operator would ask everybody but Aunt Rula to hang up so the two parties could hear each other, but the operator herself always stayed on the line; news traveled faster than television in this fashion.

My memories of this period are particularly keen. It was such a great change in my life, from city to farm life. And while I did miss many of the comforts of my life in Cincinnati, I loved that farm, and the old iron pump that gave us water, and the old crank phone in my auntie's kitchen that brought my far-away father home to me. These were truly my own "good old days."

Wanda Burkhart
Prescott Valley, Arizona

Mother's Aprons

I am blessed with a treasure of wonderful memories of growing up in the 1920s;
among them is the memory of my mother's aprons.
Behind their skirts I found a haven of love and security as I made my way
through the fears and tears of my childhood.

I shut my eyes and recall the wonderful feel and smell of a freshly starched apron,
and all of its special uses. It had corners to dry a tiny tear, and pockets that often
held magical surprises. It made a basket, to carry fresh vegetables from the garden
or a few chips of wood to build a warm fire. In the lap of an apron I could bury a
sad face, heal a hurt, or sit quietly to say my good-night prayers.

My mother's aprons were homemade, the result of afternoons of searching
through patterns and shopping for fabric at the general store—and then hours of
cutting, hand-sewing, and fitting. Each dress had a coordinating apron or two. A
good apron covered well, was long, comfortable, and easy to put on and take off.
(A dirty apron was often quickly replaced by a fresh one at the first sight of
company.) And an apron was necessarily well-starched. Mother made her own
starch by cooking cornstarch or flour into a paste and then dipping
her aprons into it. Good housekeepers never made lumpy starch.

The era of the apron is over; aprons today are novelty items, not part of a
woman's everyday uniform. But the memory of my mother's apron will always be
with me, a symbol of her love and care through the years of my childhood.

Bette Cole
Pioche, Nevada

In the early forties, a mother's job of feeding her family was made more difficult by government-imposed rationing of meat, cheese, butter, coffee, and sugar. Government stamps were required to buy any of these staples, and the stamps were both hard to come by and confusing to redeem. The American mother, however, was undaunted; in 1945, in the midst of rationing, Americans bought and consumed more food than at any time in history.

To the old-fashioned American farm family, home and work were one and the same. Up with the first light in all four seasons, and in bed shortly after dark, the farm family of the twenties and thirties lived a simple, timeless existence. Their isolated world was disrupted, however, by the spread of the automobile and the advent of mechanized farm machinery, both of which helped push the farm family abruptly into the modern world.

The Crunching Snow

Strange how a sight, a sound, or a smell can stir the memory
and call to mind times and places far away. Recently, on a frigid winter day,
the sound of snow crunching and squeaking under my feet took me back to
childhood. There I was, some sixty years ago, on our farm as dusk descended.
I was following my father out of the cheery warmth of the kitchen
into the frigid world of winter. It was evening chore time,
time for milking, for throwing bales of hay down from the mow,
for bedding down the animals warm and comfortable, and for battening down
the barn and sheds for the cold, dark night ahead.

Stars twinkled overhead as we trudged single file down the narrow path
from the house to the barn, with only the feeble lantern light dancing on the
snow around us. The air was still, but sharply cold—a cold that stung the nose
with needle-sharp pricks and numbed the toes as it penetrated scarf,
coat, black-ribbed stockings, and long underwear.

When we reached the barn, the golden light of our lanterns streamed into the
open door and glowed around us, while strange shadows lurked in familiar
daytime corners. Inside was warmth, radiating from the farm animals, and the
blended smells of straw, oats, and still-fragrant dry hay; of horses and cattle; of oil
and harness leather; and of warm milk as it squished and foamed into pails.

The cattle lowed contentedly. A horse whinnied at a familiar sound.
It was nighttime on the farm; the stars looked very close in the black-velvet sky,
and the snow crunched and squeaked under my feet.

Jeannette K. Olson
Granite Falls, Minnesota

MEMORIES OF FAMILY

remain with us always, memories of lessons learned from Mother in the kitchen and evenings gathered around the radio, of Grandma's button box and joyful summertime reunions.

Memories

Gus Kahn

Egbert Van Alstyne

Mem- o - ries, Mem- o - ries, Dreams of

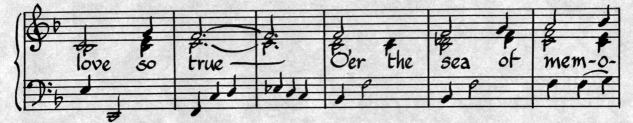

love so true — O'er the sea of mem-o-

ry I'm drift- ing back to you — Child- hood

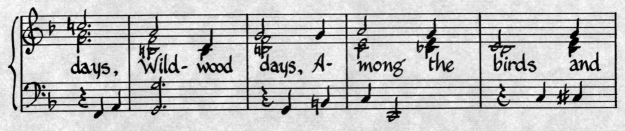

days, Wild- wood days, A- mong the birds and

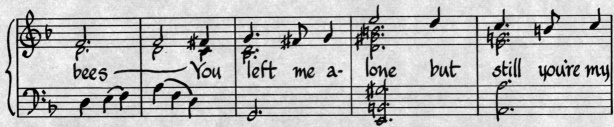

bees — You left me a- lone but still you're my

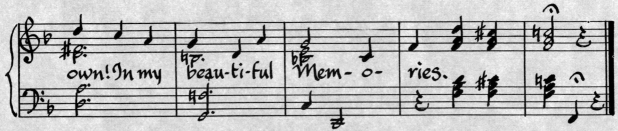

own! In my beau-ti-ful Mem- o - ries.

Mama's Pie

I was nine the summer Mama taught me how to bake a pie. It was an occasion, a rite of passage, a journey back into family history.

"You take this much flour," Mama said, dumping an undisclosed amount in a large bowl, "then you add shortening—about this much." She dropped a gob of sticky white stuff into the flour. "Now a pinch of salt. Take this pastry cutter and cut through the flour and shortening until it looks like cornmeal." I had no idea what cornmeal looked like, but I kept cutting, certain Mama would give me a hint when it got to the right stage. After a bit, she looked at it, nodded, and announced it was time to add water.

"You never dump water into pie dough," she warned. "You sprinkle it on, a tiny bit at a time. Use your hand, like this." She dipped her fingers into a cup of water and shook the drops over the mixture, tossing it now and then with a fork. When the dough could be pressed into a crumbly ball, she took half the mixture out of the bowl and pressed it together into an oval on the floured board. "Now you roll it out, but only roll it once," she said. "Pie crusts are like people—treat them gently and they'll turn out tender, but if you keep pushing and pressing them, they'll turn out tough and tasteless every time."

Gently, we transferred the flattened dough into a pie plate. "Now the berries," Mama announced. The wild blackberries, frosted with sugar and flour and seeping with purple juice, tumbled into the waiting shell. After I rolled the top crust, Mama cut a curved line across its center. "Just like my Mama used to do," she murmured. She crimped the edges with her finger and thumb and brushed the top with cream. We slipped the pie into the oven, and Mama put on the teakettle—a sign we were to have a talk. When the cups were filled and steaming, Mama pulled two chairs up to the table and we sat. For the first time, I sensed that Mama and I were somehow equals, and I felt special, privy to some feminine world I had never known before. Mama stirred her tea and started to talk.

"We were poor," she said, "but we never knew it. Daddy and Mama raised ten of us on a small farm. We always had fresh vegetables, milk from the cow, and plenty of eggs, even during the depression. And Mama always made pies. There were green apple pies and pumpkin pies, even mincemeat. But our favorite was always wild blackberry pie. We kids called the berries 'little creepy crawlers' because the vines crept along the forest floor, tangling themselves around stumps and over stones. We'd clamber through the prickly vines searching for the sweet, dark berries; we ate as many as we saved, staining our fingers and lips with the purple juice. My mother baked the pies as soon as we returned with the fruit."

"Is that when you learned how to bake pies, Mama?" I asked. "Yes," Mama said, her smile soft with remembrance. The fragrance of the baking pie wound around us, casting a smell of homey intimacy as we sipped our tea, sharing our heritage until the timer interrupted us with a rude buzz. As we removed the pie from the oven, Mama sighed with satisfaction and said, "There's a job well done." I knew she meant more than the baking of the pie.

Pam Kennedy
Honolulu, Hawaii

The proper way to make a wild blackberry pie is just one of the lessons of the kitchen passed down through generations of American women. Since 1932, a helpful tool for mothers teaching daughters has been the classic *The Joy of Cooking*. First published in that year by a private publisher, the cookbook has become a part of almost every American home, helping pass the traditions of the kitchen from mother to daughter to granddaughter.

American women have always used their sewing skills to make clothing for their children, equipping them with everything from snowsuits for winter play to suits and dresses for Easter Sunday. President Roosevelt called upon such such sewing skills to serve the larger, American family. The WPA hired women to turn surplus Army coats into clothing for the children of families on relief.

Snowsuits

When I was a child, my dad worked at the local paper mill in White Pigeon.
This gave him access to worn mill felts as they were replaced on the giant rollers.
To the owners of the paper mill, these felts were unneeded waste;
to my dad, they were warmth and comfort for his children.

Each summer, my father's sister, my Aunt Gertrude, traveled by train to our town
to stay with her mother. And each year her sewing skills outfitted my sisters and
brothers and myself with new winter clothes. She and my father dyed the mill
felts a dark color, pressed them, and cut them into patterns.
"Stand still, let me mark the hem," Aunt Gertrude would mutter through a
mouthful of shiny, silver straight pins. It was hot and miserable fitting the
snowsuits on those humid summer days, but the excitement of the bright gold
zippers, the leggings with suspenders, and the knitted ribbing at the wrists and
ankles—all the signs of a real snowsuit—made it bearable.

The felts never wore out. We ran and rolled and sledded through the snow,
remaining always warm and dry. As we outgrew each suit, it was passed on to a
sibling or cousin. They in turn passed them along again,
making my father's original gift timeless.

Now, many years later, I glance toward the racks of winter coats and snowsuits
in the department stores, and the snowsuits of my childhood,
made from simple, discarded material transformed by the love of my father and
aunt, come back to mind. I realize that times really have changed,
and that I was one very lucky child.

Phyllis M. Peters
Three Rivers, Michigan

Nineteen thirty-four was a difficult year for farmers. Record cold snaps in the winter followed by searing summer heat resulted in one of the most devastating droughts ever to hit the American heartland. President Roosevelt did what he could to help, signing the Farm Mortgage Refinancing Act and the Federal Farm Bankruptcy Act, both aimed at saving American family farms from foreclosure.

The Art of Loading Hay

Fifty years ago we harvested hay in the old way, with a mowing machine and a rake with large iron wheels. Haying was long and tiresome, extending from late June well into August, the hottest days of the year. Yet those were also days of contentment and satisfaction. I enjoyed riding behind the team of grays, and I loved the solace of the sun.

When the timothy cured, the rake, with its curving, clanging tines, left long windrows across the meadow. With brawn and pitchfork, we transformed the windrows into haycocks and hauled them to the barn.
I don't remember my age when my father decided it was time I learn the art of loading loose hay. Loading wasn't easy for a boy; binding it on to the wagon to make it secure required strength and skill and experience. Of all places for my lesson, my father selected the steepest hill in the fields.

All went well, and when the first load was on the wagon, I started the team for the barn. Suddenly, the load slid off the rigging into a tangled, twisted mass on the downhill side. I dug myself free from the bulging mound and sheepishly climbed back on the wagon. I expected a strong reprimand as my father struggled to pull the hay apart and pitch it back onto the wagon, but he never said a word. His silence was certainly out of character, and I wonder now if he, too, might have met the same fate loading his first hay, perhaps in that very same field.

I still occasionally spot an old mowing machine or hay rake, rusting in tall weeds by an abandoned barn, or by a stone wall, overgrown with bushes and vines. They bring back fond memories of the peace and serenity of August meadows speckled with haycocks at sundown, and the loving lessons of my father.

Lansing Christman
Welford, South Carolina

Grandma's Button Box

My grandma was a seamstress;
She earned her wage that way;
And though she's long retired,
She sews most everyday.
She always carries with her
A thimble and some thread,
A tiny pair of scissors,
And a needle that she says

Will come in very handy
In case, by some surprise,
The need to do some mending
Might suddenly arise.
My grandma has some things
She's piled up through the years—
Odds and ends of fabrics,
Old patterns she holds dear.

But the things she has the most of,
Or so it seems to me,
Are buttons by the boxful,
Which she adds to constantly.
"I need a button sewed on!"
She often hears us say,
And off to get her button box she
Bustles straight away.

It seems she has a million
Of every size and hue;
She even has some buttons
Shaped like little cubes!
While some of them are wooden,
There are others made of brass,
And some are even antique,
I think made out of glass.

I'm sure that there's a story
For each button in that box,
Recalling all the things she's made
From coats to party frocks.
So if you need a button,
Don't buy one in a shop—
Until you first have looked inside
My grandma's button box.

Coleen L. Lewis
Lovell, Wyoming

Old-fashioned buttons are now a popular collectible, probably because almost everyone has memories of a mother or grandmother sewing. And every serious seamstress had a button box. In the thirties and forties, many buttons were still finished by hand-painting or carving, making them quite valuable to collectors in today's world of mass-production.

Homemade taffy is almost unheard of today. This is not surprising, for taffy requires a truly physical effort on the part of the cook. To make taffy, along with the sugar and butter, be sure to have a pair of strong arms, or as many small and eager young arms as you can gather—for only the anticipation of a child will make the pulling seem effortless.

The Taffy Pull

In my mind's eye, I can picture Grandma's kitchen as though it were yesterday once more. Sweat-beaded windowpanes, a pot on the stove filled with a much anticipated boiling concoction, and the combined aroma of vinegar and sweetness drifting through the air. My cousins and I licked our lips and grew more and more impatient by the minute: the taffy was cooking! When Grandma finished, she poured the liquid taffy onto a greased cookie sheet and cautioned us against touching it until it had cooled enough for pulling. Finally, the sweet-sour delicacy was ready; we went at it with a vengeance. We strained our tiny hands and arms, pulling and stretching the wonderful, sticky mass. When the taffy became light in color and hard to pull, we knew the moment we had waited for had arrived. Grandma cut it into small pieces and passed one to each child. Our patience and hard work were rewarded by the delightful flavor. Ah, sweet memories.

I still have Grandma's recipe, and although I can never recreate the childish wonder of those afternoons in her kitchen, I can almost recreate her taffy. Two and a half cups of sugar, a half cup water, a quarter cup vinegar, the tiniest dash of salt, and a single tablespoon of butter, all heated over medium heat in a small pot. I heat until the soft-crack stage, and then take it off the stove and add a teaspoon of vanilla. At this stage it must be handed over to the children for pulling. I always remind them to grease their fingers, but they seem to like the way the taffy sticks as they pull it, just as I did. They pull and pull and I recognize the strain and the anticipation. When it becomes light in color, and simply too difficult for them to pull, I know it is ready. Just like Grandma did, I cut it into small pieces and reward the children. To them, it is as wonderful as it was for me as a child, and I love seeing the reflection of my own childhood in their happy faces.

Phyllis Carr Johnson
Chesapeake, Virginia

In the days when every woman knew how to sew, every little scrap of fabric was put aside for use in some future project. The most common use for scraps was a patchwork quilt, but women experienced with needle and thread could create almost anything out of the pieces in their sewing basket. This pillow transforms discarded ribbons and braids into a colorful accent to the living room sofa.

Old-Fashioned Ribbon Pillow

This pattern was originally made from leftover scraps of ribbon—colorful pieces that may have once adorned a daughter's ponytail or a special dress. Woven into a pillow top, these mementoes of special times and special people are preserved in a beautiful and practical way.

Choose fourteen designs or colors of one-inch wide grosgrain ribbon or woven braid, each cut to one yard long. The combined width of all ribbons and braids must be fourteen inches to cover the pillow top.

For the pillow, cut two fifteen-inch square pieces of cotton fabric. Run a basting stitch a half inch from the edge on all sides.

Cut one ribbon in half; set aside one half and place the other on the right side of one fabric square. Beginning about two inches from the end, pin the ribbon to the fabric, aligning the edge of the fabric with the basting line. The short ends of the ribbon will overlap the edge of the fabric. Making sure that the ribbon lies flat and straight, baste it to the fabric along top and bottom edges.

Cut a second ribbon or braid in half; set aside one half. Pin the other half next to the first ribbon, edges touching lengthwise, top and bottom even. Baste at top and bottom. Continue pinning and basting the ribbons to the pillow top, arranging them to create a colorful pattern and completely covering the area within the basted square. Repeat process with second halves of ribbon pieces, this time weaving the ribbons in and out of the ribbon pieces already attached and repeating the color and design pattern established.

Stitch along basted line through ribbons and pillow front fabric. Pin raw edge of eyelet one quarter-inch from edge of pillow front. Baste, turning ends under.

With right sides together, pin pillow back to front. Stitch one half-inch from edge, leaving a ten-inch opening on one side. Trim seams, clip corners, and press seams open. Turn right side out. Insert pillow form and slip stitch opening.

Alice Clark
Chelsea, Massachusetts

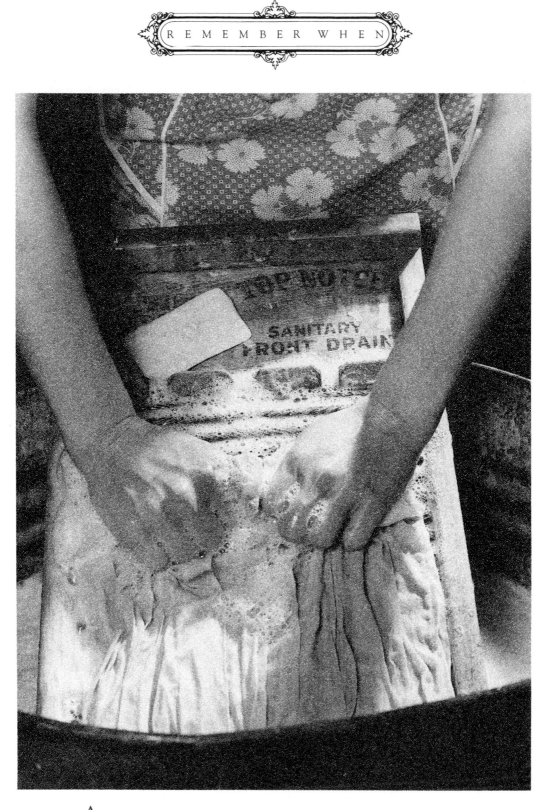

Automatic washing machines were common in the thirties and forties; but in isolated rural areas, families still washed by hand one day a week, and they still relied on the old-fashioned washpot and washboard to get their clothes clean. But washing was neither a solitary or pleasureless chore; the common task brought together families and neighbors for shared work and socializing.

The Washday Picnic

We got an early start, but the sun was already heating the air when we arrived at the spring. The wagon was loaded with a washpot, two laundry tubs, and a washboard. It was a hot, dry summer; and since our well barely produced enough water for cooking and drinking, we went to the spring on washdays.

Grandma and Grandpa were already there. Grandma was shaving a bar of lye soap into a washpot and Grandpa was carrying water up from the spring. As soon as our wagon stopped, we sisters climbed out and ran to the water. In a pool just below the spring, a jug of milk was completely submerged; but what caught our eyes was a big green watermelon settled down beside it.

We started a fire and began the wash. First the whites were put into the pot to boil, then the print dresses and other colored things, and finally the men's overalls and work shirts. We carried the hot clothes from the washpot to the tub with a broomstick. After rubbing them on the washboard, we rinsed them and hung them over low bushes and on barbed wire fences to dry.

We ate lunch and rested in the shade while the clothes dried—fried chicken, crowder peas, cornbread, and milk. After lunch we girls wandered off to wade in the water. Grandpa called "if someone will fetch the knife, I'll see if this watermelon is ripe." We ran to oblige, and watched expectantly as he stuck the point of the butcher knife into the end of the huge watermelon and brought it slowly around to the center. The melon gave a loud pop and split open revealing a bright red pulp. We bit into the crisp, sweet meat. Soon the juice was running down our chins and elbows, but the taste was worth this little discomfort.

The rinds were fed to the mules and then we folded and packed the clothes and hitched up the team. It was time for the family to head home to evening chores.

Elva Kennedy
East Prairie, Missouri

The Charlie McCarthy Show

During the heyday of live radio in the thirties and forties, families gathered together in the living room to listen to exciting and timely broadcasts, including FDR's famous "fireside chats," the suspense of *The Saint*, and numerous comedy hours.

Sunday nights at eight o'clock held the most appeal for many American families. With the evening dishes cleaned and neatly stacked and the children's toys in their proper places, Father settled into his comfy chair and the family gathered around in anticipation of another hilarious episode in the lives of Edgar Bergen and Charlie McCarthy.

The duo was not actually two people as the name implies, but a ventriloquist and his dummy. Bergen played the role of the calm and patient adult defending the values of his society, and Charlie, his wooden sidekick, portrayed the saucy, pleasure-seeking teenager. Their routine usually consisted of Bergen attempting to teach Charlie the ways of the world and proper etiquette—always with disastrous results. Edgar's soft, paternal words of sense and experience fell on deaf wooden ears. Their banter was usually carried on through plays on words, with Charlie tossing out stinging asides now and then about Edgar's thinning hair and moving mouth.

Families all across America tuned in to the show each Sunday night; its simple comedy was a delight to a nation struggling through economic hardship and war. With Charlie McCarthy, Edgar Bergen taught us all that it was possible, and wonderful, to laugh at ourselves.

Kathy Halgren
Milwaukee, Wisconsin

Franklin Delano Roosevelt's "fireside chats" were a highlight of radio programing in the thirties. Heard in living rooms across America by families gathered together around the radio, these quiet, homey speeches soothed the nation's depression fears and worries and won support for the President's New Deal.

Sunday Afternoons

From days of youth I still recall
Our Sunday afternoons . . .
The lazy, peaceful, tender times,
The old-time gospel tunes.

With mother at the old piano,
We all would join in song,
And often neighbors would drop in
To join a sing-along.

It was carameled-apple time,
With cake and ginger ale—
A time to chat in calm repose
Or tell an olden tale.

Sometimes Dad read a Bible story
Or Mother read from Grimm's,
Or tic-tac-toe took up our time
While the log grew dim.

Each Sunday afternoon brought time
For neighborly good cheer,
For family fun, and fireside talk:
Good times, undimmed by years.

Craig Sathoff
Iowa Falls, Iowa

Charles Darrow of Germantown, Pennsylvania, invented the game of
Monopoly in 1933 as a means of supporting his family during the depression.
Darrow hand made game sets and sold them himself door to door. In 1955,
Parker Brothers bought the rights to produce the game, and today it is played
in over twenty-seven countries and in fifteen languages.

Family Reunion

Grandpa's on the ladder, painting,
Finished with the lawn,
Clipped the sidewalks, pruned the hedges,
Busy since the dawn.
Grandma's washed and waxed the kitchen,
Made up extra beds,
Now this much-too-quiet dwelling
Waits for joy ahead.
Kids are coming home this weekend,

All the cousins, too,
Rock these rafters with new vigor,
Of a laughing crew.
Grandpa loves it, every minute,
Not a breath to spare,
Wants to store up lots of memories
When the family's there.

Dan A. Hoover
Hillsboro, Illinois

In the twenties and thirties, the automobile created a new mobility in American society. This proved vitally important during the depression, when jobs were often a long way from home. As a result of this new-found mobility, however, families found themselves suddenly split apart, making the tradition of the family reunion more meaningful and popular than ever.

Since the beginning of the century, photography has been accessible to the general public, and photo albums have become a part of American family tradition. In the twenties, Kodak came out with the Vest Pocket camera, a new, compact model in an array of bright colors, the more feminine of which came with matching lipstick. Compared to today's models, these "compact" cameras were anything but— too large for a vest pocket or any other.

The Family Album

In our home we have a treasure
Tucked away within a drawer;
It's a faded family album
Which we call "Our Memory Store."
In its pages there is hidden
A part of life now gone,
Which is ours to love and cherish
As the days and years move on.

Many evenings during winter
When the wind is wild outside,
We will gather at the fireside
With our album open wide,
To live again a wedding day
Or a picnic Mom arranged;
Then perhaps turn pages leisurely
Amazed at how we've changed.

Though its pages number many
With quite a few now showing wear,
To us each year enhances
Warmth and love now pictured there,
For the beauty of remembering
We could never ask for more
Than our treasured family album
Tucked away within a drawer.

Roy Zylstra
Minneapolis, Minnesota

A crocheted picture frame not only shows off a favorite grandchild, it makes use of a good, old-fashioned skill. Crocheted afghans, slippers, hats, scarfs, and baby clothes were once a part of every American home.

Capture a Moment

Nothing captures a memory better than photographs; they bring past generations to life and preserve family heritage for the future. I keep favorite family photos in crocheted picture frames that add a personal touch to my family treasures.

The frames are simple and inexpensive to make. Gather together two ounces of white, four-ply knitting yarn, a size G crochet hook, a metal ring three inches in diameter, twenty-seven inches of ⁵/₁₆-inch ribbon, three miniature imitation roses, a small amount of imitation baby's breath, and two plastic pearls. You will also need a hot glue gun and a glue stick. Choose the colors of ribbon and roses to coordinate with the photo. Once the materials are together, it only takes a couple of hours to complete a perfect showcase for your most treasured photos.

Make 72 single crochet in ring. (Opening will be approximately 2¹/₂ inches.)
Join with slip stitch in first single crochet. Chain 1, single crochet in same stitch.
Chain 3, skip 2 single crochet, single crochet in next single crochet. Repeat around.
Join last chain 3 in first single crochet. Break yarn and weave end securely.
You should have 24 chain 3 loops.)

*To make the back of the frame, chain 6 and join to first chain. Chain 3. (This counts as one double crochet.) Make 17 more double crochets in ring. Join with slip stitch in top of chain 3. Chain 3, double crochet in same place, 2 double crochets in each double crochet around (36 double crochets). Join in top of chain 3. Chain 3, 2 double crochets in next double crochet, *1 double crochet in next stitch, 2 double crochets in next double crochet.* Repeat around directions within *. Join with slip stitch in top of chain 3. Break yarn and weave in loose end (54 double crochets).*

Once the crocheting is complete, begin to assemble the frame. Weave the fifteen-inch ribbon piece in and out of chain 3 loops. Glue ends together on back with glue gun. Place photo on the back of the front piece so that the image is centered; glue the back piece to front, being sure that both right sides are showing. Make a small bow with the twelve-inch ribbon piece and glue to top of frame along with pearls and roses. The frame can either be hung with a small piece of ribbon or displayed in a small easel on a table top.

Peggy Pease
Frostburg, Maryland

SCRAPBOOK OF FRIENDS

full of memories of those who have touched our lives,
of cherished dolls and games of marbles in the old schoolyard,
of messages written faithfully in an autograph book
and letters penned in true devotion.

Toyland

Glen MacDonough   Victor Herbert

Toy - land! Toy - land! Lit-tle girl and boy - land, While you dwell with- in it — You are ev - er hap - py then. Child- hood's joy - land, Mys- tic mer- ry toy - land! Once you pass its bor- ders, you can ne'er re- turn a- gain.

The Rain Barrel

When I was a little girl, there were no television programs to entertain children, but there were rain barrels: magical, enchanting places in our own backyards where our simple playtime dreams came to life.

As I recall, our summers were blessed with frequent soft, warm rains, which constantly replenished the contents of our rain barrel, keeping it almost always full and running over, and making marvelous puddles to splash our bare toes in as we stretched ourselves as tall as we could in an effort to gaze into the barrel's watery depths.

The little boys sailed tiny boats over the bounding waves; we girls dipped our pitchers full of soft rain water and ran off to make a batch of fresh mud pies. The water was usually warm from the sunshine, and best of all, there was no need to worry about spilling—outdoors, the water could do no harm.

Riding around our countryside the other day I glimpsed a rain barrel on the corner of a farmhouse and was delighted to see a group of little tots splashing in its water. Apparently at least a few children in today's world of television and video games understand the magic contained in a simple rain barrel.

Helen Colwell Oakley
New Milford, Pennsylvania

A simple wooden rain barrel is an unlikely plaything, but for children living on isolated farms in the twenties and thirties, store-bought toys were a rarity, and playmates were often limited to siblings. Thus the ordinary objects of the farmyard, including the rain barrel, became fantasy lands limited only by the child's ability to imagine.

It is unfortunate that marbles have fallen out of favor with American children, for the game has been a part of our history since the country's beginnings. The games of marbles that little boys and girls enjoyed in the twenties, thirties, and forties were the same games played by such great Americans as Abraham Lincoln, Thomas Jefferson, and George Washington.

A Doll of Yesterday

We found her in an auction box
Bought at a sale last fall;
The contents: books and linens,
And a lacy, silken shawl.

Underneath a cardboard cover,
To our complete surprise,
We found a doll of yesterday
With brown curls and bright blue eyes.

Her dress was hand-stitched tafetta,
Trimmed in ruffled ivory lace.
Her bonnet of blue velvet
Framed a dainty, porcelain face.

We wondered just how old she was
And what her name should be
Then looking at her crinkled skirt
We solved one mystery.

In lettered fine embroidery,
Small stitches barely there,
Jenny Lee, her name was shown,
Tiny letters, but still clear.

How many children played with her
And curled her long brown hair?
How many in a hundred years
Have rocked her in their chair?

Which children held her tenderly,
Who owned and loved her well?
Jenny Lee sits in a rocking chair
And smiles, but will not tell.

Elisabeth Weaver Winstead
Nashville, Tennessee

The one-room schoolhouse is a truly American tradition. While exclusive private schools were flourishing in Europe, Americans held fast to their belief in free public education for all children. The no-frills environment of the one-room schoolhouses found in small towns across the nation provided American children with the basic training their parents believed was the key to success.

One-Room Schoolhouse

It was called Forest Dale School, Junior, a white frame, one-room schoolhouse down the lane from where the original one-room log schoolhouse our parents had attended still stood.

Guarding our schoolhouse were a few bayberry bushes that had withstood the rigor of years of countless innings of baseball and endless winter snowball fights. The grass around the school yard was worn almost to extinction by daily games of tag and marbles and crack the whip, by round after round of tug of war and fox and geese, of anthony-over and London bridge, and by the ceaseless pounding of little girls' feet as they played at jump rope.

Each morning, the teacher arrived early, and while we children played in the yard she kindled the fire or saw to some grading. She called us through the double front doors with a few sharp rings on her small handbell. Inside, thirty desks of graduated sizes were arranged in rows facing one large desk for the teacher. A coal heater occupied the corner by the smallest desks. A splendid map case hung over the upper grades' blackboard, helping us imagine far away places.

We all walked to school in those days, carrying dinner buckets as well as books. Once inside, we began our day with the Pledge of Allegiance, followed by the Lord's Prayer. Pupils in all eight grades did their lessons together—there was no other way with only one teacher and one room. But we all learned what we needed, maybe more easily than today's students, who have to deal with all the distractions of modern schools and modern methods.

Lucile Wilson Adams
New Lexington, Ohio

My Autograph Book

My autograph book is a treasure
Written by many a friend;
And I often pause to read it
From the first page through the end.

Its pages are chapters of memories,
Friends that I've left behind,
But their messages I cherish
And their words bring me peace each time.

Esther Johnson
Woodville, Wisconsin

Many adults treasure an autograph book as a reminder of the joy of their teenage years. The term "teenager" origniated in the forties, when post-war peace and prosperity created a generation of carefree young people with time and money to spend. The music industry, clothing manufacturers, and advertisers of all kinds directed their attentions to this suddenly important segment of American society.

The Magic of a Letter

A letter came from you today
And though you are so far away
It was as if you held my hand
And somehow made me understand.
Such magic in a page or two
Brought joy to thrill the heart anew;
Like carrying on a friendly chat
About old times, our own shared past.

Your letter brought real joy to me,
Like joining hands across a sea
Of time, and seemed to bring back to my door
The joy of seeing you once more.
Small wonder then, that I should wait
To see the mailman at my gate
And hope that he will bring once more
Some old-time happiness to my door.

Carice Williams
Riverside, Illinois

The twenties, with great improvements in the postal service, saw an amazing boom in letter writing. In 1900, nearly four billion stamps were sold in America. Twenty-two years later, that number had more than tripled. But while the postal service had modernized, electric typewriters were still a thing of the future; letters were either written by hand or typed on an old-fashioned manual typewriter.

As more and more Americans moved into the cities to look for work, weekend trips to the country became quite popular. A picnic by a country lake with good friends was the perfect remedy for the strange new stresses of city living.

An Old Friend

I met an old friend yesterday,
A comrade from the faraway,
And glad I was his smile to see,
For this is what he brought to me:

The school house from the Long Ago,
The boys and girls I used to know;
The little home on Sibley Street
Where all the youngsters used to meet;

The games we played, the things we did,
The secret places where we hid,
The pranks of all our youthful crew,
The punishments we sometimes drew.

A living book, he seemed to me,
Fresh from memory's bindery;
A book whose leaves were edged with gold
So many merry tales he told.

Who meets an old friend on the way
Meets all the joys of yesterday;
The laughter which he used to know
And all the charm of long ago.

Edgar A. Guest

The friends made in youth are often those who remain forever in our hearts, for their names and faces are reminders of simpler times, when football games, ice cream sodas, and senior proms were our most pressing concerns.

I'll Let My Heart Return

There's sweetness in the word "return"...
Today I long to go
To an old familiar place
My childhood used to know.
The landscape seems more lovely there
In sweet-remembered charms
And I feel the hills reach out
With smiles and loving arms
To bring me back across the miles
And equi-distant years
To daisy-dotted meadows
That never heard of tears.

Of course, it's home I'm speaking of;
And for dear friends I yearn.
And though I'll not be going back,
I'll let my heart return.

— June Masters Bacher
Escondido, California

RECOLLECTIONS OF THE NEIGHBORHOOD

*fill our hearts with joy and longing for a simpler time,
for summer evenings on the front porch and familiar faces on
the street below, for an ice cream cone from the old drugstore
and a beautiful dress from the five and dime.*

Take Me Out to the Ballgame

Jack Norworth   Albert Von Tilzer

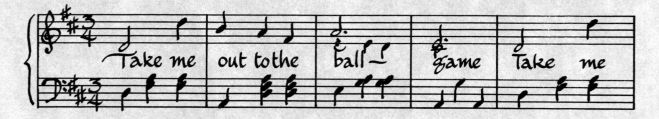

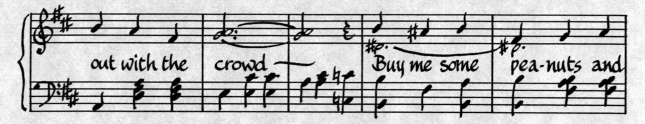

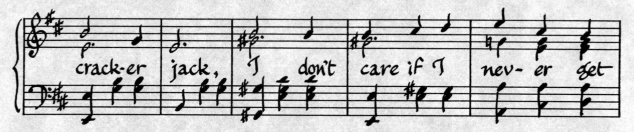

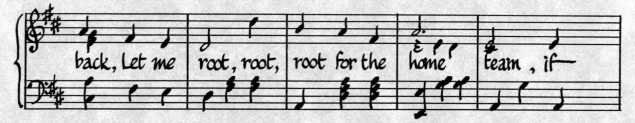

69

The Old Porch

I remember summer evenings
And the old porch swing,
With all the warm nostalgia
That childhood memories bring;
The street lamps gently flickered,
Casting shadows on the grass,
As the family sat and chatted
And watched the people pass.
The fireflies in the cannas
Made spangles in the dark,
While just around the corner
We could hear a hound dog bark.

There were happy calls from children
As they wandered home from play,
And the crickets chirped softly
In a summer roundelay.
That's why an evening's twilight
Sets me to remembering
Those sweet and tender moments
I spent in that old porch swing.

Mary Ellen Stelling
Atlanta, Georgia

The front porch is a truly American phenomenon. In European houses, a porch is an enclosed or sheltered entranceway; but in the American home, the porch is out in the open, both to catch the hint of breeze on a summer's night, and to provide a perfect viewing platform for the action of the neighborhood. In the thirties and forties, before air-conditioned living rooms, most families spent hot summer nights on their front porch.

Familiar Street

Give me the time to savor well
The taste of home and friends,
The time to thrill my senses with
The thrill their nearness lends.
Each house, each shrub, each dog and cat
I'll want to pause and greet;
It seems each tree has strings to me
Along Familiar Street.

The world won't see the paths I do,
The signposts and the turns;
But when they're walked day after day
A person sort of learns
The angle to the grocery store,
A short-cut to the park,
Where bulging walks might trip you up,
The hazards after dark.

But best of all, the well-worn paths
My inner eye restores
Are those, in memory, between
My own and dear friends' doors.
Oh, some I've trod in aproned style,
Sometimes in party gown,
And often when our paths would cross
We'd "talk" new ones downtown!

It brings a smile and quick-drawn breath
To know that soon my feet
Will walk among those folks of mine
Along Familiar Street.
Give me capacity to hold
The friendliness of "here,"
To share its warmth with someone else
Who finds his going drear.

Somehow there are no strangers left
Among the ones I greet
When friendship paves remembered ways
Back to Familiar Street!

Esther Kem Thomas
Lebanon, Indiana

Familiar faces in the old-fashioned neighborhood were not limited to the people who lived next door. The policeman walking his beat, the iceman and the milkman making their daily deliveries, and the lamplighter on his nightly rounds were all a part of the fabric of the neighborhood.

The first self-propelled combine appeared in 1938. For three years previous, American farmers had been enjoying the increased productivity of a tractor-driven combine. The new combine took them one step further. With one machine, farmers could now cut, thresh, and clean grain. This proved especially helpful during the war, when the demand for their grain was greatly increased.

The Threshing Ring

Although I appreciate our advanced methods of harvesting today, I remember fondly the "good old days" of the old-fashioned threshing ring, when harvesttime brought the neighborhood of farmers together through the special bond of common labor.

The neighborhood men would meet to decide who would be the grain haulers, the bundle loaders, the unloaders of the great sheaves of wheat and oats, and who would man the threshing machine. Together they would travel from farm to farm, helping with the harvest. It was quite a thrill for us kids to see the black engine on giant wheels puffing coal black smoke chugging into our barn lot, pulling the separator behind it. When all was set up, the bundle loaders fed the sheaves of wheat or oats into the jaws of the separator, which shivered and shook the grain out into the grain wagon, where we small children jumped and danced barefoot in the sea of oats.

As I grew older, Mother needed me in the kitchen along with the other neighborhood women to help fix dinner for the working men. We set pans of warm and soapy water and linen towels out under the trees for them to wash before coming in to our feast—usually two kinds of meats with all the trimmings, vegetables from our own gardens, pies, cakes, salads, coffee, iced tea, and homemade bread.

These were good times of fellowship and working together. Now a single man can run a big combine alone, perhaps even unload and haul the grain himself. Times sure have changed, and I miss the rich heritage of friend helping friend and neighbor helping neighbor on the farm.

Rosemary Carter
Russiaville, Indiana

Grocery Boxes

Time was when grocers received their supplies in wooden boxes. So naturally, our groceries were brought home in boxes—none of the paper sacks and plastic bags that we see today.

Grocery boxes made carpenters of every kid. Add a motor, a few boards, and some wheels to an apple box, plus a length of rope for a steering gear, and you had a dandy race car. Boys put wheels on the boxes, added a tongue, and hitched up the dog. It took a little coaxing for the dog to pull this new cart, but patience and a bit of praise usually did the trick. Girls made dollhouses, with dad or big brother pressed into service to help with the building.

Most kids had a puppy or a small dog who, of course, needed a house. The children sawed and hammered and nailed and presto! Fido had a house. Maybe a little lopsided and crooked, but the dog never seemed to mind. There was no end to the uses we found for those boxes. Then came the cardboard era. Cardboard was fun to play with for awhile, but it wasn't much good for building things. Now everything comes in paper or plastic—no good at all for playing or building.

We always had something to entertain ourselves with in those days, and I think we had more fun with our homemade creations than we did with anything store-bought. All that was needed was a hammer, a saw, a few boards, and some nails. Add a little ingenuity, and surprises were sure to come!

L. Gordon Stetser, Jr.
Pipestone, Minnesota

The neighborhood grocery store was replaced in the twenties and thirties by a new phenomenon—the chain supermarket. Piggly Wiggly was the first to experiment with the idea for these giant grocery stores, hoping that volume-purchasing, smaller payrolls, and self-serve shopping would translate into lower prices and more customers.

While to their parents it may have been simply a pharmacy, to children of the thirties and forties the neighborhood drugstore was a magical place. As small children they brought handfuls of pennies to buy their favorite candy or an ice cream cone; and as teenagers they met friends at the drugstore soda fountain, away from home but still safe in the confines of the neighborhood.

Double-Decker Ice Cream Cone

When I was a child, a chocolate and vanilla double-decker ice cream cone was a special-occasion treat; this delicious concoction still holds a magical appeal.

Coming from a large family—the twelfth of thirteen children— I wasn't accustomed to more than the basic necessities of life. Once in awhile, however, good fortune would come our way, and Mama would send my brother and me to the drugstore for ice cream cones. One such trip remains vivid in my mind. It was winter, and snow had been falling most of the day. Taking the sled along on our trip seemed like a good idea; I got to ride. As my brother pulled the little sled along the quiet, moon-brightened streets, I watched the spectacle of lights in the clear winter sky. The moon, with its mournful face, looked right at me, and each one of the millions of stars sparkled clear and bright. The snow on the ground glistened and made crunching noises under my brother's adult-size galoshes.

Cantor's Drugstore was small and compact; every inch was put to good use. Floor-to-ceiling, glass-encased cabinets held bottles of liniments, cough elixirs, and disinfectants; boxes of bandages and gauze; and barrels of softly-scented soap. A soda fountain occupied one side of the room, and two little marble-topped tables with wrought-iron chairs stood in the corner. I sat in one of these chairs while Mr. Cantor filled our order.

Mr. Cantor was a soft-spoken, slightly bald man of middle age. He filled our cones with large, bulging scoops of creamy chocolate and vanilla ice cream, carefully wrapped them with several layers of napkins, and placed them securely in my hands as I climbed aboard the sled for the ride home. Mama was at the door waiting, and she held the cones as we took off our heavy winter clothing. As I sat in the parlor, settled deep in the soft cushions of the old horsehair sofa, I felt safe and loved. It was a blessed feeling, one that I still feel every time I have a chocolate and vanilla double-decker ice cream cone.

Mary Theodore Skarmeas
Danvers, Massachusetts

The 5 & 10¢ store has gone the way of the neighborhood grocery, the victim of large chain stores. But in the thirties, many a small child's dreams came true in these magical stores, which stocked luxury affordable even to depression-burdened families.

The Green Silken Dress

I shopped the 5 and 10¢ store today. I shop there frequently, not always making purchases, but always recapturing a golden moment from yesteryear.

As was the custom when I was a girl, every Saturday night our family made the six-mile trip into town in our old car to purchase the week's groceries and any other necessities. I say "necessities" because times were hard; the country was just recovering from the Great Depression, and very few families had money for extras. But we didn't always go entirely without; when shopping was completed, Dad always stopped and bought ice cream to eat on the trip home.

One Saturday night, while my Dad and brothers passed the time watching the trains come and go at the railroad depot, my mother, little sister, and I shopped at the 5 and 10¢ store. While looking through one of the racks of clothing at the back of the store, I spied the green silken dress. What a coincidence! Just weeks before I had admired the exact same dress on a classmate; how I had wished to have one just like it, to wear to Sunday school and to church. But the price, I feared, was out of reach: $2.98. I didn't say a word to my mother, but she must have seen the way I looked at that dress, the way I fingered its green silky fabric. Without a word, she took the dress from the rack, walked to the counter, and placed it there as if she were buying a sack of flour or a warm winter hat—a necessity.

I suppose Dad stopped for ice cream that night, just as he always did, but all I can remember is the joy and thankfulness that filled my heart as I clutched my green silken dress. Many years have passed since then, but the 5 and 10¢ store still retains its ability to capture my heart, for it is there that I learned the depths of my mother's love.

Loise Pinkerton Fritz
Lehighton, Pennsylvania

The few true old-fashioned general stores that remain are tourist attractions, relics of a past era. Department stores and malls have made the one-room stores, packed to the ceiling with every necessity and run by a man or woman who could locate any given item in an instant, obsolete.

The General Store

Among my favorite memories of when I was a young girl is the old-time general store. The "Roaring Twenties" were just beginning to make themselves heard in America, but in our small village, country life was still quiet and peaceful, and to a small child, stepping into the general store was stepping into a world of dreams.

To this day I recall the enchantment of the sights and sounds and smells that captivated me; with only the slightest effort I am a child again, entering the store with my mother on a cold winter's day. I hear again the door creaking open; I feel the rush of warm air meeting the frigid cold; I see the farmers standing around in woolen macintoshes, snow dripping from their four-buckled overshoes onto the oiled floor as they consider the weather, the price of grain, and the neighbor's new team of horses. The mingled smells were a conglomerate that only an experienced visitor could sort out: freshly ground coffee from the red mill; tea from India; spices from the Orient; boxes of shiny red apples; the bright, fragrant, "only at Christmas" oranges; tropical yellow bananas hanging over the counter; burlap bags of brown potatoes, smoked sausage, and cheese. All these blended with the acrid smell of tobacco and kerosene cans, the pungency of calico dyes, and the strong, unmistakable scent of leather.

On one side of the store was the dry goods counter, with round stools where children could spin around until dizzy while their mothers sorted through the bolts of flannel and dress material or selected buttons, lace, or embroidery floss. Shelves displayed hand-painted dishes and ordinary blue speckled enamel-ware. The store had everything we needed—everything a child could imagine wanting.

Today, children shop with their parents at giant malls and shopping centers, full of stores that hold treasures I could not have dreamed of as a child. But with all that excess, I wonder if today's children can ever know the wonder I felt every time I walked through the doors of our general store

Jeannette K. Olsen
Granite Falls, Minnesota

REMEMBRANCES OF HOMETOWN

bring peace to our hearts, filling our minds with thoughts
of band concerts in the town square and movies
on Saturday nights, of the excitement of the circus parade
and the magic of the carousel at the country fair.

Alexander's Ragtime Band

Irving Berlin

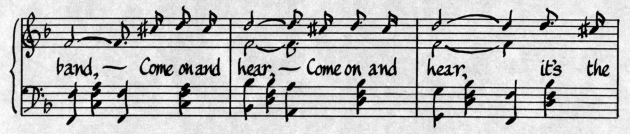

Come on and hear, ── Come on and hear ── Al- ex- an-der's rag-time

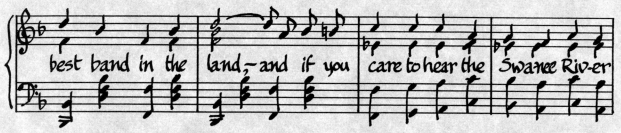

band, ── Come on and hear, ── Come on and hear, it's the

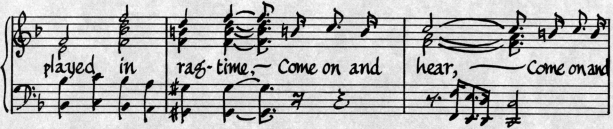

best band in the land,── and if you care to hear the Swanee Riv-er

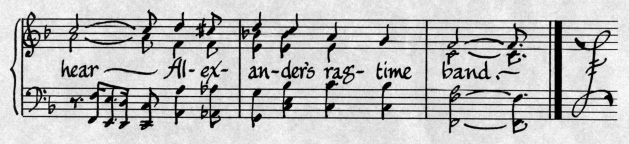

played in rag-time, ── Come on and hear, ── Come on and

hear ── Al- ex- an-der's rag- time band. ──

The first town clock was erected in New York City in 1780 at the Old Dutch Church. As the country grew, more and more town squares featured a giant clock that not only served as a reliable timepiece, but also as a cherished local landmark.

The Old Town Clock

The old town clock in the old town square
Still high and lofty stands;
'Tis century-old with ample time
Still on its well-worn hands.

It has ticked away the moments,
Chimed hours one by one;
Its round face is weather-beaten
With years of rain and sun.

It's out-lived the horse and buggy
While overlooking all;
It has reigned through wars and tumults,
Seen great men rise and fall.

Yet with dignity of purpose
It goes on, fearing naught;
To the faithfulness it's rendered
It goes on without a thought.

'Tis century-old with ample time
Still on its well-worn hands.
The old town clock in the old town square
Still true and faithful stands.

Georgia B. Adams
Reading, Pennsylvania

A trip to town on Saturday night often ended with a visit to the hometown movie theater. In the thirties and forties, movies became big business in America, drawing people from the countryside, small towns, and big cities alike with visions of a beautiful, fantasy world free of the fears and cares that worried the nation.

Saturday Nights

Years ago, Saturday nights were special and truly enchanting. Little towns and villages all over America perked up and came to life as evening set in, with a steady stream of traffic, busy sidewalks, and lights flickering all up and down the main street. On every other night of the week, towns and villages went to bed when the sun went down; but on Saturday night downtown was full of folks come to do their shopping, see a movie, stop for an ice cream at the drugstore, or enjoy a barn dance at the local grange hall.

Most everyone dressed up to go into town on Saturday night. The ladies and young girls were so pretty in their best outfits of ruffles, full petticoats, and swirling skirts; the gentlemen too were neat as a pin and well-polished in their white shirts and black ties, glistening after a weekly scrubbing.

My sisters and brothers and I drove into town with Mom and Dad in our shiny black Buick. As we circled down Pierce Creek Road we caught our first glimpse of the town, all aglow with street lamps. The stars twinkled up above and a full moon lent its soft light to the rolling hills of the countryside. We seldom went into town except on Saturday night, so on our occasional daytime visits, the town seemed strangely quiet, lacking the glitter of its weekend-evening self.

Those Saturday nights of long ago are still fresh in my memory—the stepped-up tempo of the little villages and towns as the lights flickered until midnight, the folks hustling happily around the square, and the music from the barn dance drifting through the streets. How I miss those magical Saturday nights!

Helen Colwell Oakley
New Milford, Pennsylvania

The Old-Time Movie House

The architectural grandeur of the movie theaters of the 1940s made going to see a movie like dining at the Ritz; today, seeing a movie at a modern cement-block, multi-screen low-rise is more like a quick stop for fast food.

In the forties, movie theaters created a feeling of glamour and elegance—an atmosphere of Hollywood make-believe. These theatres were large and cavernous, with vaulted ceilings, ornate, celestial murals, and gold leaf carvings covering the walls. Crystal chandeliers hung in the lobby and plush red carpeting covered the floors and aisles. The powder rooms were expansive and comfortably furnished with upholstered chairs and sofas. Gilt-edged mirrors and soft lighting added to the charm. Seating capacity varied, but the larger of these magical movie houses held two to three thousand people.

In stark contrast, the movie theater of the nineties is a study in efficiency: long, low buildings with basic rectangular construction, filled with anywhere from three to fourteen narrow screening rooms, most of which hold only between fifty and one hundred people. The floors are sticky, the seats uncomfortable, and the lobbies and restrooms strictly utilitarian.

In my childhood, the movie house was a central and distinct feature of downtown; today, theaters have moved to the suburbs, and are found not on Main Street, but inside giant malls or isolated beside some superhighway. Today's movie theater is just another stop in our busy days. In the forties, the theaters, and the movies they showed, created an atmosphere of make-believe. They offered the movie-goer a complete afternoon in a world apart, not just two hours of fast and efficient entertainment.

Mary Theodore Skarmeas
Danvers, Massachusetts

The grand movies of the thirties and forties required grand settings. Old-time movie theatres were works of art themselves, with every detail a part of the experience. New York's Roxy held 5,000 people; the Capitol even more. Recognizing that the atmosphere of the theater was part of the draw of the movie, theaters vied with one another for the distinction of the most extravagant and most luxurious surroundings.

The Band Concert

Summer band concerts were a part of my small-town growing-up years. Each Thursday afternoon, the old bandwagon rolled uptown into a wide open area of Main Street. As the day wore on, people began to drive uptown and park in the spaces in front of the bandwagon. People without cars walked into town after their evening meal; farm families arrived still later, with produce to barter at the grocery store. All the stores were open, but the drugstore fountain, the ice cream parlor, and the popcorn and peanut wagon did a particularly brisk business.

Finally, around eight o'clock, the band members assembled and began a concert of marches, overtures, and popular tunes. There were also instrumental and vocal solos by local celebrities or talented visitors. Occasionally, Mr. Meeker, our band director, treated the crowd to one of his spirited slide trombone solos. After each number was finished, there was applause and a honking of horns by the appreciative audience.

The concert continued to the final number, always *The Star Spangled Banner*. Children who had raced through the streets all evening, hardly hearing the band, were somehow attuned to our national anthem. It was a signal for them to run to prearranged meeting places to rejoin their families for the trip home.

Ours was a small town band made up of citizens of every age. I eventually became a member myself, following in the footsteps of my brothers and sister. I could hardly wait to collect my pay after my first concert—a big, round shiny half-dollar. Yes, grade schoolers started out at fifty cents and, if they stayed long enough, eventually made two dollars. We played because we loved to play, and because we loved those special Thursday nights.

Eleanor J. Brown
Ottawa, Illinois

Today, bands are usually only heard at halftime of football games or in high school auditoriums. In the early decades of the century, however, things were different. The weekly band concert was a major event in town, and almost every city or town had its own band made up of local citizens.

The tradition of religious revival meetings goes back to the very beginning of America. The zeal and fervor that marked the preaching at revival meetings in the twenties and thirties is the same that moved Puritan congregations three hundred years earlier.

That Old-Time Religion

I'd like to go just one more time
To a good old-fashioned meeting;
Where your neighbors slap you on the back
With a warm and friendly greeting.

Where preacher knows The Word by heart
And prays when he feels like praying.
His sermon isn't typed and read:
He says what he feels like saying.

I'd like to sit on an old-time bench
And feel that old-time preaching
Warm my heart, and my neighbor's heart
With the Good Lord's old-time teaching.

I'd like to sing those old, old hymns
That I don't need a book for singing,
With the old pump organ blasting out
Till it sets the rafters ringing!

I love my church with its formal airs
And its modern pews for seating;
But just once more I'd like to go
To a good, old-fashioned meeting.

Blanche Hines Zapert
Edgewater, Florida

Named after a festival held yearly on Lake Chautauqua in New York, Chautauqua brought big-city entertainers and speakers to small-town America. Chautauqua traveled to ten thousand towns, reaching forty million citizens, and made the people living in isolated rural areas feel a part of the social and cultural life of their nation. Teddy Roosevelt was a big supporter of Chautauqua, calling it the "most American thing in America."

Chautauqua!

Chautauqua is coming next week! The news thrilled everyone—children, parents, and grandparents, too. Our family packed up and spent a week at our cabin on the lake, where the speeches and shows would take place. A huge circus tent was erected on a large open space in the center of the assembly grounds, and benches were positioned before a stage. There were to be two shows daily, and we went to every one, hearing the best speakers, the finest singers, and even a few politicians and preachers. In the mornings there were special events for children and talent contests for the spectators.

For families like us, who lived in America's rural villages and towns, Chautauqua was a taste of the city; it let us in on what was going on in America, made us feel special. William Jennings Bryan came to town one summer, as did beautiful actresses from Broadway and famous musicians. In the sleepy summer life of our small town, the signs announcing the coming of Chautauqua spread a spirit of excitement throughout the community. For one week, at least, our small town was to be a grand and important place!

Ellouise Halstead
Union Grove, Wisconsin

Circus Days

Circus days are coming soon;
Candied apples and balloons!
Clowns will wear their funny faces
And big red shoes with fat shoelaces.

Lion trainers with their hoops,
Acrobats and loop-de-loops!
Popcorn, peanuts, cracker jack
Will add pleasure to their acts.

Big top laughter loud and clear,
Is the happy sound you'll hear.
Circus days are filled with fun,
For the old and for the young.

Kay Hoffman
Johnstown, Pennsylvania

July 16, 1956, was the end of an era for the American circus. On that date, Ringling Brothers and Barnum and Bailey Circus performed their last show under the big tent. Rising costs had forced the show to move indoors.

Up until 1930, country fairs and amusement parks flourished in America, and so did the wood carvers who made horses for the carousels. In those days, each horse was handmade and distinct. The depression, unfortunately, wiped out the majority of carvers, and the carousel, now full of identical, mass-produced horses and animals, has never been the same.

The County Fair

On a wonderful day like today,
There's a glorious sun in the sky,
And a rainbow of colors is seen
Where banners are flying high,
And the cries of laughter and mirth
Ring out from the carousel
As we gaze at the jubilant crowd
And the sights too wondrous to tell!

There's enchantment wherever we go
Down the length of the gay midway,
Where pink cotton candy is spun
And popcorn is on display.
The barkers wait to entice us
To seek after a beautiful prize,
To reach for the blue of heaven
On a thrilling, spinning ride.

There are champion roosters and hens
And thoroughbred horses and cows;
There are frolicking lambs and calves
That draw large, admiring crowds.
There are whirlagig birds and balloon,
And sights too wondrous to tell,
But what makes it a wonderful day
Is our ride on the carousel.

Joy Belle Burgess
Milwaukie, Oregon

SOUVENIRS OF TRIPS

*are the memories we cherish of a special time at grandmother's
house or the very first ride aboard a steam locomotive,
of the old-fashioned simplicity of a covered bridge
or a glimpse of the future on the Pennsylvania Turnpike.*

My Merry Oldsmobile

Vincent Bryan

Gus Edwards

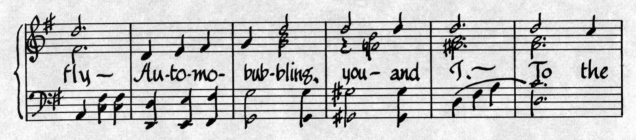

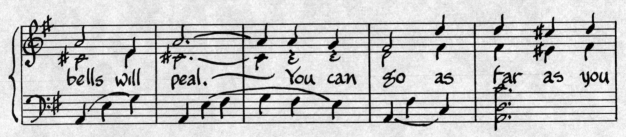

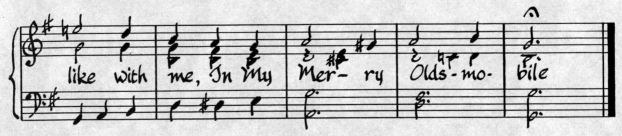

Fifty years ago, it was not unusual for a grandmother to take care of her grandchildren. Before the age of fast and easy air travel, families lived together, or at least close by, and roots were not something people searched for, but the very foundation of their lives.

A Visit to Grandma's

When I was a little girl over a half-century ago, one of the most exciting times of all was a visit to Grandma's. In the winter, she lived with Grandpa in a large white house with green trim in the city; in the summer, she moved to another large white house with green trim, this one in the country. How wonderful it was to visit Grandma and be the center of attention for a brief spell. I was one of ten children in our family, and although I always felt loved at home, it was pure heaven to visit Grandma's and be spoiled occasionally.

Understandably, Mom was often too busy to have us underfoot when she was scurrying around the kitchen preparing large breakfasts, lunches, dinners, and suppers; but Grandma was less busy, and more indulgent. She seemed to enjoy having little helpers to set the table, ice the cakes, lick the bowls, and sample goodies. We loved it when she would send us to the store on errands—either just around the corner from her city home or a short walk down a dirt road from her country home. Sometimes we ran to the store for Grandma several times a day, and almost every time she would give us a few pennies or a nickel for candy or an ice cream cone.

While at Grandma's we went on numerous trips—to the cemetery to hear her speak of relatives from long ago, to family reunions, to barn dances, to church suppers, and to ice cream socials. No wonder I treasure those long-ago memories of my first trips away from home; for the destination was a place as warm and welcoming as the home I had left behind.

Helen Colwell Oakley
New Milford, Pennsylvania

By the twenties and thirties, America's covered bridges had begun to disappear. The first covered bridge was probably one built in 1805 over the Schuylkill River near Philadelphia. The bridge was covered at the suggestion of a local judge, whose estate looked out over the river. He sought a more pleasing view, and asked that the conventional bridge be covered by handsome siding and a roof.

The Old Covered Bridge

The old covered bridge lingers on affectionately in my remembrances of the nostalgic times of a long-ago America. "Clippity, clop, clop, clop. Clippity, clop, clop, clop," the horses hooves would echo as wagons, buggies, and sleighs entered the old covered bridge, and then "rumble, rumble, rumble" reverberated through the stillness of a sleepy countryside.

The old covered bridges lent an aura of magic to old-fashioned country scenes. Some were rather plain, put together with rough, unfinished lumber, while others were quite beautiful with planed siding, shingled roofs, smooth plank flooring, and several tiny windows. Streams gurgled underneath, peaceful and placid, or fierce and terrifying during a sudden storm.

On a moonlit night, it was truly enchanting to ride into a covered bridge in a sleigh or carriage. The moonbeams crept through the cracks between boards and the panes of the tiny windows and danced on the inside, bouncing off cars and carriages carrying young lovers. Outside was the open countryside, breathtakingly beautiful under the twinkling stars. Today's cars and superhighways get us where we are going faster and more reliably, but what I wouldn't give for just one more ride through an old covered, country bridge!

Helen Colwell Oakley
New Milford, Pennsylvania

The Old Steam Locomotive

I remember the steam locomotive
That chugged-chugged its way along
The tracks on the way to the city—
It had quite a rhythmic song.

I'd smile at the friendly old conductor
As he collected the tickets with care;
My Daddy was seated beside me
Oh, all of the fun we did share!

And the loud toot-toot of the whistle,
It seems I can hear it yet;
The power of my fond old memories
Will not let me forget.

I remember the steam locomotive
Way back when the days were slow;
Say now, do you share my memories,
Did you ride on that train long ago?

Georgia B. Adams
Reading, Pennsylvania

A quarter of a million miles of railroad tracks crossed the nation in 1916, the peak of the train's popularity as a means of travel and of its importance in trade and industry. In the twenties and thirties, the railroad system began to decline, leaving many with only memories of the excitement and romance of the old steam locomotive.

Trains

From my darkened room I heard the early morning train sound its whistle. The train was still far from my house, but the soft call of the whistle echoed through the countryside and easily covered the distance to my room. Trains don't come through town much anymore—and the sound of this pre-dawn whistle stirred my memory.

The first time I ever rode on a locomotive, our family was going to another town to visit friends. Instead of driving, my father decided to take us all on the train. For days I was so overcome with excitement that I hardly ate or slept. My mother grew weary of my constant "how much longer till we go" inquiries. The day of the trip, I was up early, nervously waiting at the station for the sound of the approaching train. My anticipation was heightened by the familiar, far-away tune of the train whistle. The tracks gleamed in the morning sun; my eyes followed them into the distance, where the distorted image of the train finally appeared.

As the powerful moving body of energy approached, my blood quickened its pace through my veins. The very ground I stood upon trembled beneath my feet. There was a screech and a squeal as the wheels braked for a stop, and a huge sigh escaped from the engine as the train finally came to a halt, as if it were glad for the chance to rest.

The conductor placed a step stool on the ground so that we could easily reach the narrow doorway, and we entered and walked down an equally narrow aisle, so narrow that if two people met going in opposite directions; they were forced to turn sideways and brush past one another. The train moved in a swaying, rocking motion. Houses and farms outside my window took on a new dimension. I heard the familiar whistle, but this time I was a part of it, privy to the secret world it announced to those outside. Today, I cannot hear that whistle without going back to that first train ride, without a surge in my heartbeat and the urge to run and feel the earth quake at the coming of the train.

Sally Frankowski
Warsaw, Indiana

In American ficiton from the beginning of the century, a popular image is
that of the young country boy or girl venturing to the city for the first time,
usually by train. In the first decades of the century, trains helped make
America a truly united nation by connecting rural areas, big cities, and every
small town in between.

The Old Green Line

Weekly we'd board the "Old Green Line"
And on to Chicago we'd go;
Dancing for Sis, piano for me—
It was lesson time, you know.

Soon a second fare was due
As we crossed over the state line;
Three cents was all it cost for Sis
But for me it was a dime.

In summer—hot; in winter—cold,
And the car swayed side to side,
But none of this mattered to Sis and me
Entranced by this magical ride.

Finally, on one snowy day
We read an ominous sign
That said "last trip on Sunday":
It was the end of the old Green Line.

Lillian Helmcke
Calumet City, Illinois

In the early 1900s there were 20,000 miles of streetcar track in the United States. By World War I that number had increased to 45,000, with 11 billion passengers riding streetcars each year. The streetcars changed the course of history by making city jobs accessible to suburban dwellers, beginning the age of commuting. After World War II, streetcars began to fall out of favor, losing out to the more economical and flexible bus and subway.

Chicago World's Fair

The year was 1934 and my twenty-year-old husband and I were going to the World's Fair in Chicago. The country was in the throws of the depression, so we were on a very limited budget; but with one hundred dollars from my grandpa and our little Ford Roadster, we set out from our home in Florida full of anticipation.

The drive was long and tiresome, but our visions of what was ahead kept us going. We took turns at the wheel and talked and sang and slept our way across the hundreds of miles of roads that separated Florida from Chicago. What a dazzling sight met our eyes when we finally arrived at the fair grounds! We roamed about until our feet were sore and aching. We viewed all the free exhibits and picked up a few inexpensive souvenirs; one evening we even managed to have dinner at the cafe where Sally Rand was performing her famous fan dance. This shocked us a little, but it made us feel worldly and sophisticated. Ah youth! What a tireless and enthusiastic time it was. For three days we stayed at the fair, up with the dawn and out all day, taking in all that we could. Just when we thought our money had run out, we had a stroke of good fortune—Mother wired us twenty-five dollars through Western Union, with the message, "Stay and have another day's fun." And we did.

The drive home took two and half days, and we drove straight through. Once home, it was back to work and chores and everyday life. But we had brought back a priceless souvenir from Chicago and the World's Fair, despite our limited budget—we had our memories.

Mary Ellen Stelling
Atlanta, Georgia

In 1932, a trip by car from Florida to Chicago to see the World's Fair was not unusual. The automobile was transforming American life, and advertisers moved to cash in. The Burma Shave Company was one of the most successful. Their campaign of brilliant roadside billboards—six red signs spaced one hundred paces apart along the side of the highway—made company slogans impossible to ignore, or forget.

By the late thirties, there were 23 million cars registered in the United States. The automobile, including the demand it created for steel, rubber, and other products, was the country's biggest industry. The automobile also gave many American consumers their first taste of buying on credit. In the twenties, three out of every four cars were purchased on time, often consuming three quarters of the buyer's monthly salary to meet payments.

The Old-Fashioned Car

An old-fashioned car is a handsome thing,
And a parade of such beauties will always bring
So many sweet memories quickly to view,
Memories of yesterdays and happy times, too.
I'll never forget the old-fashioned car,
Nor the roaring or rattling or head-bouncing jars
When the skinny-heeled "lizzie" hit the big ruts
Of an old country lane full of rocks and deep cuts.

And I'll never forget the fun of a ride
When rain whipped the isinglass curtains aside,
And water came splashing all over our faces
And the windshield was nothing but rivery laces.
At times the old car would get balky and stall;
There was no automatic starter at all.
But with some turns of a crank the car roared with a jolt;
It vibrated and screeched at each connection and bolt.

Then the driver adjusted the gas and the gears
And took off with a racket that deafened our ears.
We laughed and we sang, the car's noise compiling,
At twenty-mile speed we thought we were flying!
We made Sunday visits to folks here and there
And went on some picnics and to the big county fair.
We followed the trails that were old wagon traces
And rode with the wind pushing hard on our faces.

Yes, the old-fashioned car was an exquisite thing,
And it made the proud owner feel like a rich king
As he sat stiff and straight, the wheel gripped tight;
He hung onto that wheel with all of his might!
The seats had coil springs; how we bounced on the bumps
When the car dropped in holes or ascended the humps.
Traveling by car in the old-fashioned days
Was rough and uncomfortable in a few dozen ways.

And it was with good reason; those old roads were rough.
But the old car could take it; it was built good and tough.
Those cars proved their worth in many harsh ways,
And they stir up fond memories of long-ago days.

Helen Shick
New Bethlehem, Pennsylvania

The Pennsylvania Turnpike

Today, everywhere we go it seems we travel on superhighways—four lanes, maybe even eight, of straight black asphalt surrounded by trees and divided by a grassy median. It's a bore, so much so that we look forward to taking the "scenic route," traveling down some old, two-lane road winding through the countryside, through small towns and open farmland. How things have changed.

When I was six years old, car travel was only by those "scenic routes," and drivers dreamed of better, faster, more reliable roads. The new Pennsylvania Turnpike was to be the fulfillment of those dreams. I remember my mother and father talking about how much more quickly we could drive to grandma's house in Bedford from our home in Carlisle, and how much safer it would be, traveling the smooth straight road the government promised.

I listened to my parents talk and wondered what a turnpike would be like. One Sunday in October of 1940 I found out. We packed a picnic lunch and my brothers and I piled into Dad's old black Buick. We got on the turnpike right near home in Carlisle. We had to stop and take a ticket from a man inside a booth before we could drive on the turnpike, almost like going to the movie theatre. Dad said our money would help pay for the road. I imagined such a road must have cost a king's fortune; it was straight and long and smooth, surrounded by trees, with the most perfect soft green grass in the middle of two sets of concrete lanes. We drove for a few miles, then Dad pulled over to the side of the road; we had a picnic right there in the grass, with traffic passing by on each side.

My parents still live in Carlisle, and often when I visit I take the old turnpike, much the worse for wear and no match for most of today's highways, but always a reminder of another time, when travel in the "fast lane" was something unusual.

Zachary T. Rivers
Jericho, Vermont

The Pennsylvania Turnpike ushered in the age of the superhighway in America. Although the Turnpike was not the first four-lane, limited-access highway—the Merritt Parkway in Connecticut and the Bronx River Parkway in New York came first—it was the most celebrated, inspiring in Americans visions of a united and powerful nation connected by a series of fantastic roads.

MEMENTOES OF FIRST LOVES

are held close to our hearts, from the notes of a favorite popular song to keepsakes held safely within a hope chest, from the cherished memory of a first dance in a country barn to Grandmother's locket held tightly on wedding day.

I Love You Truly

Carrie Jacobs-Bond

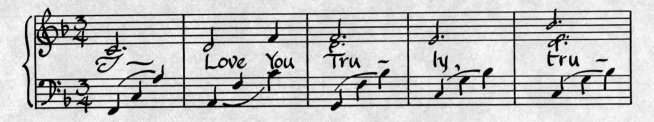

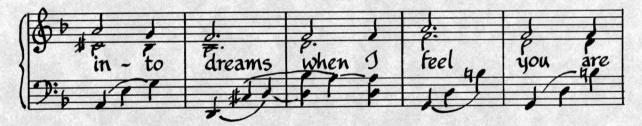

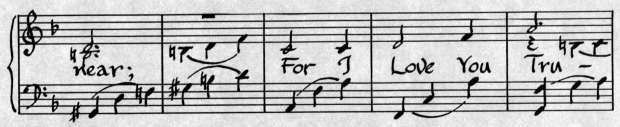

Hope Chest

Her hopes and dreams and wishes
Were placed within that chest
Along with lovely handiwork
And quilts, the very best.

Pillow cases, linen towels,
And coverlets were there;
An afghan made by Grandma
And doilies crocheted with care.

She'd added, too, some photographs
And awards from grade-school years,
Some books with treasured autographs
And mementoes she held dear.

She tucked them away and waited
For that extra special day
When her very own Prince Charming
Would whisk them both away.

Craig Sathoff
Iowa Falls, Iowa

Quilting goes back to the ancient Chinese, who first discovered that fabric gained warmth and durability when stitched in quilted layers. The art of quilting, however, was refined by American women, who turned piles of scrap fabric into warm, durable, and beautiful coverlets. Although hand quilting is a rare art today, in the early part of the century a handmade quilt was a basic requirement for a young girl's hope chest.

Box Social

The metal bands on the wagon wheels made sharp musical tones as they broke through the icy crust of the snow. The horses pranced in the cold air, eager to get moving. Dad had filled the bed of the wagon with hay and all of us climbed in, covering ourselves with quilts. The event was a box social in the neighborhood one-room schoolhouse. It was the winter of 1921.

When the people had all arrived, a program prepared by students and teacher began. Recitations, dialogues, and pantomimes had all been practiced for weeks. The show finished with fiddle music played by a neighborhood man.

After the program, tension mounted as the food was prepared for auction. The boxes were elaborately decorated with colored tissues and other odds and ends. No one was supposed to know the owner of each box, although some of the girls cheated and told their latest heartthrob which box was theirs. The men bid cautiously, eager to get the box of the girl of their dreams, but also fearful of getting the wrong one. After each box was sold, the couples spread out around the room to eat their suppers. I imagine that many a wonderful romance began on these nights of simple hometown entertainment.

May Perry Geyer
Onaga, Kansas

The one-room schoolhouse was more than just the location for daytime instruction. In small towns across America the little red schoolhouse served a number of community purposes, including such much-anticipated events as the box social.

Square dancing is a distinctly American form. It developed in the country's early days, the compilation of French quadrilles, Irish jigs, English reels, and American regional flavors. Although the country barn dance has all but died out today, square dancing is kept alive by a large population of devoted Americans.

Country Barn Dance

With jingle of bells and beat of hoof,
Fragment of song and a lusty hail
For each bright pane or snow-heaped roof
Glimpsed over drifted hedge or rail,
The big sleigh, drawn by a sturdy team,
Comes to a stop by a tall barn door
That swings to admit a swirl of steam
And a tide of youth to an ample floor.

Homeward bound in the straw-filled sled,
The horses slowed to a jingling walk,
Each girl resting a sleepy head
On her partner's shoulder—there is no talk
While yet the shuffle of dancing feet,
The wail of fiddles, the caller's tune,
And the haunting quest of the waltz repeat
The night's new glory, and love's old rune.

Dana Kneeland Akers
Superior, Wisconsin

Old Tunes

Dainty music on a rack;
Waiting there, it seems,
Gentle hands to bring it back
From the realm of dreams.

Once it fashioned mood and pace;
Lifted spirits high;
Filled a gay important place
In a time gone by.

Music, too, grows old, you see;
Sleeps, and wakes to start
Echoes, tuned to memory,
Deep within a heart.

Ruth Jenner
Seattle, Washington

Each phonograph sold by the Victor Talking Machine Company bore the instantly recognizable trademark of a small white dog listening intently to the sounds coming from a giant wooden speaker. Englishman Francis Barraud designed the trademark after observing his brother's fox terrier puzzling over a voice coming out of the machine. The logo was also used by a British Company, now known as EMI.

Oh, *Promise Me* is a classic American love song. With words by Harry B. Smith and music by Reginald de Koven, the song, originally sung as a part of the operetta *Robin Hood*, has become a traditional part of many American weddings.

Oh, Promise Me

The Big Band

The "Big Band Era" some folks say,
As if those days are past;
But others know the big band sound
Will not be gone that fast.

The big band groups are fewer now,
But many still abound
To lend their beat, their muted horns,
Their harmony of sound.

The big band sound has registered
A heritage of names:
Duke Ellington and Artie Shaw,
Glenn Miller, Harry James.

There's Whiteman, Dorsey, and Hampton,
There's Guy Lombardo, too,
And Goodman, Krupa, Henderson;
And this just names a few.

In fact, I think we treasure more
With every passing year
The big band sound and the fellowship
Of people it draws near.

Craig E. Sathoff
Iowa Falls, Iowa

A *New York Times* article in the thirties warned of a "dangerously hypnotic influence of swing music," which it declared was "cunningly devised to a faster tempo of 72 bars per minute—faster than the human pulse." Their warning, and that of parents everywhere, went unheeded, and the big band jazz sound swept the nation, turning band leaders like Benny Goodman and Glenn Miller into national heroes.

Something Old

I fingered the folds of my wedding gown. The silk rustled in hushed whispers, and the sparkling crystals and ivory pearls winked at me. This was the day when my dreams would become real. The little girl who had played bride in the backyard, adorned with an organdy curtain, would walk down the aisle, take the hand of her handsome young naval officer, pledge to love and cherish him forever, and begin her new role as wife. Before me, on a little table, were the traditional bridal accouterments—a pale blue silk garter, an embroidered handkerchief borrowed from my mother, a lovely new pair of pearl earrings, and my "something old," Grandma's locket.

I picked up the necklace and rubbed the smooth little heart, remembering with a smile the day Grandma gave it to me. It was my tenth birthday. I had run down to the two-room flat under our apartment house to visit the family matriarch. "You're ten today," she had finally announced after fixing me a piece of toast with butter. I nodded. "Well, I have something for you," she said in a conspiratorial tone. She went to her tiny bedroom and rummaged around in a drawer full of flannel nightgowns, cotton bloomers, and elastic stockings. "Here it is!" she announced victoriously. She came back with a floral print hanky with something tied in the corner. "Open it up!" she said, delighted with herself.

I untied the knot and slipped out the locket. "Now this," she said, dangling the golden heart from its fragile chain, "is something I want you to have. Your grandpa ordered it from the Sears and Roebuck catalogue when we hardly had enough money for food and clothes. Now you take good care of this and someday maybe you will give it to your granddaughter."

The heart-shaped locket was a symbol of the past and the future, and it became a symbol also of a special bond between Grandma and me. Now, on my wedding day, I fastened it around my neck. Grandma couldn't attend the ceremony; she was ninety years old and too frail to venture out. But I had visited her the day before and told her I would wear her locket on my wedding day. She kissed me and we held hands in silence, each recalling the past and contemplating the future.

As the organ began the first chords of *Lohengrin*, I began the walk into that future accompanied by the richness of the past, so beautifully represented by my "something old."

Pamela Kennedy
Honolulu, Hawaii

The tradition of carrying "something old" on wedding day is one that has thankfully not been lost. Although styles of wedding dress and particulars of the ceremony have changed, brides today still cherish such special possessions as an heirloom locket, just as their mothers and grandmothers did before them.

Grandma's Old Frying Pan

The wedding was over, the guests were gone,
The table was laden with gifts.
There were pots and pans so shiny and new
And linen nice and crisp.
Nestled among the modern pots
Alone and shy it did stand,
Tied by the handle with a ribbon of blue—
Grandma's old iron frying pan.

It once was new many years ago,
The day that Grandma was wed,
All through the hard years down on the farm
Her growing family it fed.
When her daughter's wedding day came
There was no money for something new,
So Grandma wrapped her most prized possession
And tied it with a ribbon of blue.

In turn the daughter's family came
And her daughter to a woman grew,
Once more the skillet was all wrapped up
And tied with a ribbon of blue.
The bride looked at all the bright new gifts,
And then, with a loving hand,
Reached for the most precious gift of all,
Grandma's old iron frying pan.

Rosa Lane
Spring, Texas

Today it might be unusual to receive grandmother's old frying pan as a wedding gift, but fifty years ago, wedding gifts were not items of luxury but of practicality. Couples starting out had usually not lived away from their parents' home before, so the most basic household items were usually the most-appreciated gifts.

Today couples often put off marriage into their thirties. Many of these same couples, however, have parents and grandparents who were married while still teenagers. Couples married at sixteen or seventeen stayed together through the trials of growing up, the hard work of raising their own families, and the challenges of old age; they truly lived their lives together.

We Have Lived and Loved Together

We have lived and loved together
Through many changing years;
We have shared each other's gladness
And wept each other's tears;
I have known ne'er a sorrow
That was long unsoothed by thee;
For thy smiles can make a summer
Where darkness else would be.

Like the leaves that fall around us
In autumn's waning hours,
Are the traitor's smiles that darken
When the cloud of sorrow lowers;
And though many such we've known, Love,
Too prone, alas, to range,
We both can speak of one love
Which time can never change.

We have lived and loved together
Through many changing years;
We have shared each other's gladness
And wept each other's tears.
And let us hope the future
As the past will always be:
I will share with thee my sorrows,
And thou, thy joys with me.

Charles Jeffreys

TRADITIONS OF HOLIDAYS

keep the past alive, from the simple knitted hat from mother at
Christmas to the beautiful flowers grown for Decoration Day,
from the family picnic on the Fourth of July
to the carols sung on the village green on Christmas Eve.

Easter Greetings

Birthday Greetings

To my Sweetheart

May this be A HAPPY New Year

WISHING YOU LUCK

THANKSGIVING BLESSINGS BE YOURS DEAR FRIEND — MAY THE DAY ADD TO YOUR STORE OF GOLDEN MEMORIES.

A Happy Thanksgiving

EASTER GREETINGS

"In glory, underneath the sod, Slumber our heroes to-day"

1861-1865

Merry Christmas

May heaven your Christmas ever bless, With all good gifts of happiness.

Shine On Harvest Moon

Jack Norworth   Nora Bayes-Norworth

Shine on, shine on har-vest moon up in the

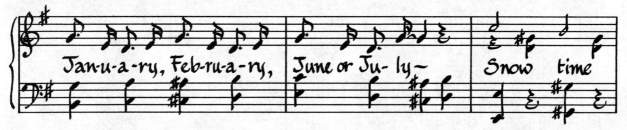

sky I ain't had no lov- in' since

Jan-u-a-ry, Feb-ru-a-ry, June or Ju-ly— Snow time

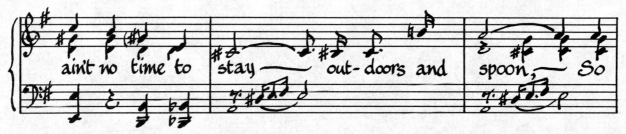

ain't no time to stay out-doors and spoon, So

shine on, shine on har-vest moon, for me and my gal.

Valentine Cookies

Yesterday my daughters came home and told me that they needed cookies to bring to the school Valentine's Day party. I scolded them gently for not telling me sooner and picked up my car keys, ready to head out to the grocery store and pick up the last box of decorated, heart-shaped cookies. But I felt a touch of guilt as I settled upon this easy solution; when I needed cookies for Valentine's Day, my mother had taken me to the kitchen and taught me to make them. Simple sugar cookies with powdered sugar frosting—every year my sister and I had sat at the kitchen table and "helped" Mother measure, mix, and cut . And every year we had home-baked cookies to hand out to our friends.

"Come on girls," I urged my own daughters, "let's make cookies." I had Mother's recipe inside the front cover of my cookbook. She hadn't written it down in the usual way—no list of ingredients and no technical sounding set of instructions. It read as if she were right there beside me, telling me just what to do.

First, beat together a third of a cup of shortening and a third of a cup of butter until they are combined and good and soft. Use your largest mixing bowl, because things are going to add up. Then add a cup of flour, three quarters of a cup of brown sugar, one egg, one tablespoon of milk, one teaspoon of baking powder, and a teaspoon of vanilla, and then just the smallest dash of salt. Beat it all again, until everything is blended. Then add one more cup of flour and mix it all up again. This has to chill for two or three hours, so divide the dough into two pieces, cover each in a bowl, and get ready to make frosting. Use a small bowl now, and mix a cup of sifted powdered sugar with a quarter teaspoon of vanilla. Add milk by the teaspoon until the frosting is smooth enough to drizzle.

The girls did a wonderful, if sloppy, job on the frosting. After doing some dishes, it was time to finish the cookies. Following Mother 's directions, we rolled the two dough sections out to about an eighth of an inch thick, and, with a heart - shaped cookie cutter (I had to make that trip to the store anyway!) shaped the cookies. Seven or eight minutes in a 375° oven on an ungreased cookie sheet, and then a few minutes at the hands of my six and nine-year-old decorators, and we had cookies—not the store-bought kind, but good, old-fashioned, homemade cookies. I hope my children enjoyed making them half as much as I did.

Vanessa Elizabeth James
Underhill, Vermont

Today, children buy packages of ready-made Valentine cards to hand out to classmates on February 14. Years ago, Valentines were always handmade, using scraps of colored paper, ribbon, doilies, and whatever else was on hand to fashion individual greetings for the holiday.

During the depression, families could often afford only one new outfit for each child in a year. In many families, that outfit was purchased at Eastertime. The beautiful new clothes made their debut at church on Easter Sunday, and then were worn for the rest of the year.

Easter Clothes

There's something about little girls at Easter
That brings a smile to my face;
I remember dressing up for the holiday
All in ruffles and my finest lace.

My small hands were neatly clad
In tiny, white kid gloves;
On my head rested a straw bonnet
To shield the Spring sun from above.

My white patent leather shoes
Were so polished they reflected
My jubilant, shiny little girl's face
When I bowed and genuflected.

I watch other little ladies now
Skipping along in their best Easter style,
And my own dear memories of a long-ago girl
Let me share in their Easter smiles.

Patra Giroux
Apple Creek, Ohio

May Day celebrations originated in England before the Middle Ages, when children would rise early on the first of May to gather flowers. The flowers, arranged in handmade baskets, were delivered anonymously to the doors of neighbors and friends. May Day celebrations survived into the beginning of this century in America, where many adults today have memories of delivering flowers to doorsteps in the early morning of the first of May.

May Day

Oh, let's leave a basket
Of flowers today
For the little old lady
Who lives down our way!
We'll heap it with violets,
White and blue,
With jack-in-the-pulpit
And wildflowers, too.

We'll make it of paper
And line it with ferns
Then hide—and we'll watch
Her surprise as she turns
And opens the door
And looks out to see
Who in the world
It could possibly be!

Virginia Scott Miner
Warsaw, Indiana

Decoration Day

Each year in late May, when Memorial Day comes around, I find myself feeling nostalgic, longing for a time gone by when Memorial Day was known as Decoration Day. This was a day truly set aside for paying tribute to those no longer with us, not just a long weekend for trips to the lake and backyard barbecues.

The days leading up to our old-time Decoration Day were busy ones. Times were hard, so instead of buying wreaths and flowers, Mom made all her own decorations. We bought crepe paper of all colors and my mother and older sisters cut and curled the colorful strips into beautiful flowers—roses, tiger lilies, mums, and many more. After the flowers were complete, they were dipped in hot wax to preserve their beauty in rain or shine. I was not allowed to cut or wax the flowers as a small child, but each year, with my mother's help, I made a pretty pink and white crepe paper bouquet to lay on the grave of a sister who had died before I was born.

When Decoration Day finally arrived, I went with Mom and Dad to the many cemeteries where relatives were buried to place our homemade flowers on their graves. Each year, I lovingly arranged my tiny pink and white bouquet on the grave of a sister I had never known.

I learned more about my family on Decoration Day than at any other time, for the holiday brought back memories of good times and loved ones to my parents. Most of the people were relatives I had never met, but on that day I felt close to them; my parents' devotion to the day made me feel that these people were my family. Today, I am thankful for that heritage.

Joyce Ayres
Elgin, Illinois

On May 5, 1866, residents of Waterloo, New York, placed flowers on the graves of Civil War dead in honor of their service and sacrifice. Two years later, May 30 was officially declared Decoration Day. After World War I the day was expanded to include American dead from all wars.

The Flag Goes By

Hats off!
Along the street there comes
A blare of bugles, a ruffle of drums,
A flash of color beneath the sky:
Hats off!
The flag is passing by!

Blue and crimson and white it shines,
Over the steel-tipped, ordered line.
Hats off!
The colors before us fly;
But more than the flag is passing by.

Sign of a nation, great and strong
To ward her people from foreign wrong:
Pride and glory and honor—all
Live in the colors to stand or fall.

Hats off!
Along the street there comes
A blare of bugles, a ruffle of drums:
And loyal hearts are beating high:
Hats off!
The flag is passing by!

Henry Holcomb Bennett
Wisconsin Dells, Wisconsin

In 1938, singer Kate Smith introduced a new song by Irving Berlin called "God Bless America." The song, and Ms. Smith, became instant American classics. In her long career, Kate Smith recorded over three thousand songs and introduced one thousand others, but in the minds of patriotic Americans, her name and voice will always be linked with the song that celebrates the nation they love.

Horseshoes used to be a common summertime entertainment, the perfect game for a Fourth of July picnic. Its popularity no doubt stemmed from its simplicity; no fancy, store-bought equipment was needed, only a few discarded shoes from the barn. And horseshoes was an ideal game for a hot summer afternoon, requiring minimal movement or physical exertion.

The Clinking of Horseshoes on the 4th of July

When I hear the clink of a horseshoe
And watch as through the air it flies
I remember the old-time picnics,
The reunions and the Fourth of July.
The Fourth was the time for meeting
On the farm with relatives overflowing;
There were grandparents, aunts, and uncles,
And youngsters to keep the fun going.
In those days great muscled stallions
Were kept for working the farms;
Always there were a number of horseshoes
Lying idle around the big barns.
Now horseshoes was a game with meaning—
It tested the wrist and the eye;
For the trick was in judging the distance

Then deciding how hard to let fly.
It wasn't a test of endurance,
Nor strenuous, too tiring, or tough;
And a man dressed in Sunday go-meetings
Could enjoy it with barely a scuff.
How we loved the clinking of horseshoes
And the thuds that meant victories;
The shouts of the winners in teamwork,
And the losers, gruff jolilities.
We have tennis, golfing, and ping-pong,
And all those games folks play on the lawn;
But there's something about lively horseshoes
That brings back the days that are gone.

Helen Shick
New Bethlehem, Pennsylvania

Thanksgiving Memories

Across the fields and woods I walked
One crisp Thanksgiving Day
To Grandpa's house for dinner
With lots of time to play.

The cold wind rattled empty husks,
A few clouds floated high;
I heard the honk and saw the "V"
Of wild geese flying by.

A cottontail bobbed down a row,
Quail roared up by the hedge;
Small chickadees flew out ahead
And led me to the edge

Of Grandpa's woods, where hickory trees
Shag-barked and tall and grey
Had dropped a crop of sweet, white nuts
Where the red squirrels play.

I kicked deep leaves of cinnamon
And heard the raucous jay
Jawing behind a white-oak grove
His music for the day.

Deep leaf mold sank beneath my tread—
A flash of tangerine;
The bittersweet and wild grape
Grew verdantly between.

I savored hickory smoke and saw
The house, the windmill wheel,
And thanked God for Thanksgiving Day
And how good it made me feel.

D. A. Hoover
Hillsboro, Illinois

Thanksgiving as we know it, on the last Thursday of November, did not become a permanent national holiday until 1941, when President Roosevelt declared it so. Before that time, the date had changed several times as officials tried to find the right number of weeks between Thanksgiving and Christmas to suit retailers, consumers, and every American citizen.

Christmas Knitting

Materials: Knitting worsted weight yarn, 300g red; 100 g white; straight needles, nos. 4, 6, & 8; no. 6 double pointed needles; two small white buttons; medium size crochet hook.

MITTENS (make 2 identical) With no. 4 straight needles, cast on 30 sts in white. Break off white and join red; work in K1, P1 ribbing for 2¼ inches. Join white. Knit 2 rows; break off white.

Shape Thumb Gusset: <u>Row 1</u>: K14, inc 1 in each of next 2 sts, K14. <u>Row 2 and all even rows</u>: Purl. <u>Row 3</u>: K14, inc 1 in next st, K2, inc 1 in next st, K14. <u>Row 5</u>: K14, inc 1 in next st, K4, inc 1 in next st, K14. Continue, knitting 2 more stitches between increases on odd rows until there are 8 sts between increases. End with purl row.

Shape Thumb: K15, place on stitch holder; K10; place remaining 15 sts on second stitch holder. Work 10 sts in st st for 7 rows. Decrease as follows: <u>Row 1</u>: K2tog across row. <u>Row 2</u>: P2tog twice, K1. Bind off and sew thumb seam.

Shape Mitten: Place sts from first stitch holder on right needle; pick up 2 sts at base of thumb; attach red. Place sts from second stitch holder on left needle; K across row. P one row. Join white; knit 2 rows. Break off white; with red, knit 1 row, purl 1 row for 12 rows. Join white, knit 2 rows, decreasing 1 st at each end of last row. Break off white.

Shape Mitten Tip: <u>Row 1</u>: K1, K2tog, K9, sl st, K1, psso, K2, K2tog, K9, sl st, K1, psso, K1. <u>Row 2 and all odd numbered rows</u>: Purl. <u>Row 3</u>: K1, K2 tog, K7, sl st, K1, psso, K2, K2tog, K7, sl st, K1, psso, K1. <u>Row 5</u>: K1, K2tog, K5, sl st K1, psso, K2, K2tog, K5, sl st, K1, psso, K1. Finish with purl row; bind off. Sew mitten and side seam.

HAT WITH EARFLAPS: With no. 6 straight needles, cast on 6 sts in red for left earflap. Knit 3 rows and work as follows: <u>Row 4</u>: K2, bind off 2, K2; <u>Row 5</u>: K2, cast on 2, K2; <u>Rows 6-11</u>: Knit; <u>Row 12</u>: K2, bind off 2, K2; <u>Row 13</u>: K2, cast on 2, K2. Continue, knitting every row until strap measures 4 inches, then work as follows: *<u>Row 1</u>: K1, inc 1 by knitting in the st below, K4, inc 1 below, K1; <u>Row 2 and all even rows</u>: Knit; <u>Row 3</u>: K1, inc 1 below, K6, inc 1 below, K1. Continue as above, knitting 2 more stitches between increases on odd rows until there are 20 sts on needle, ending with a knit row. <u>Next row</u>: K1, sl 1 as to P, K16, sl 1 as to P, K1. Knit 1 row. Repeat these two rows only 10 times more. Slip remaining stitches onto double pointed needle. *For right earflap, cast on 6 sts in red on no. 6 straight needle, knit one row, and work as given for left earflap from * to *.

Begin Cap: With no. 6 straight needles, cast on 90 sts in white. Break off white and join red; work K1, P1 ribbing for 7 rows.

Attach Earflaps: Join white; knit 10 sts. With right side of left earflap facing, hold dp needle to back side of ribbing. Working both needles at same time, knit 20 sts of ribbing and earflap together, K30, attach right earflap in same manner, K10. Knit 1 row. Break off white; work as follows: <u>Rows 1, 3, 5</u>: Knit; <u>Rows 2, 4, 6</u>: Purl; <u>Rows 7&8</u>: Join white and knit. Repeat these 8 rows 2 times more., Finish with red; knit 1 row; purl 1 row.

Shape Top: <u>Row 1</u>: With red K4, K2tog. Repeat across row. <u>Row 2 and all even rows</u>: Purl. <u>Row 3</u>: K3, K2tog across row. <u>Row 5</u>: K2, K2tog across row. <u>Row 7</u>: K1, K2tog across row. <u>Rows 9 & 11</u>: K2tog across row. Break off yarn, leaving a 10-inch tail. To finish, draw tail through remaining stitches with a tapestry needle and pull tightly. Sew back seam. Attach buttons to ear flap. With white, make pompon and attach to top of hat.

SCARF: Cast on 26 sts with red. *Knit 8 rows. Join white; knit 2 rows.* Repeat from * to *. Continue, knitting every row with red until scarf measures 32 inches. Join white and knit 2 rows. Break off white; repeat from * to *. Knit 8 rows with red. Bind off.

Make Fringe: Cut forty 10-inch lengths of both red and white yarn. Holding four of same color together, fold strands in half. Beginning at corner on short end of scarf, poke crochet hook through last row of knitting; pull folded end of strands through. Thread loose ends through folded loop. Pull until secure but not tight. Attach fringe in this manner, alternating two tassels of white, two of red across ends.

Alice Clark
Chelsea, Massachusetts

Knitting has never really fallen out of fashion, but while today it is a leisure-time hobby, it once was an inexpensive way to outfit the family for winter. A hat, a pair of mittens, and a scarf knit in bright red wool were a common sight under the Christmas tree.

The sleigh ride is a classic piece of Americana, instantly summoning images of Christmas in quaint, long-ago villages. But in rural America at the beginning of the century, the sleigh was more than simple romantic throwback, it was often the only viable means of transportation on ice and snow- covered country roads.

The Sights and Sounds of My Christmas Village

Every year at Christmastime, a vision of the enchanting Christmas village of my childhood reappears in my memories. As if by some sort of seasonal magic, I am transplanted out of time and place and find myself back in my hometown as December leads the way to the most wonderful of holidays.

There on the village green, covered with a fresh blanket of pure white snow, stands a tall evergreen, about to be majestically transformed into a most beautiful community Christmas tree. Villagers have joined together for the tree trimming and lighting festivities in the park on the village green. Children stand in wonder, their eyes sparkling with glee as trillions of colored lights pop on all at once. "There's a red one, and a green one; a yellow one, a blue one, and an orange one!" the children chorus as they try to choose the prettiest one of all! The grown-ups pause for a moment to take in the beauty of all of this, then focus their eyes on the large twinkling star shining down brightly upon a village awaiting the celebration of the birth of the Christ Child on Christmas Day.

Christmas carolers with long mufflers and songbooks enter my memories of the old Christmas village as they stroll across the green; how beautiful and inspirational their hymns and carols sound. And the organ music from the church fills the air with its magic. This is Christmas, the way I first came to know it as a child, the way it will always remain in my heart.

Helen Colwell Oakley
New Milford, Pennsylvania

AUTHOR INDEX

A 2
B 3
C 3
D 4
E 5
F 6
G 7
H 8
I 9
J 0